# Ourselves: Book 2

This split edition published 2022
By Living Book Press

Copyright © Living Book Press, 2022
Website: www.livingbookpress.com

ISBN:     978-1-922919-44-1 (Floral Cover)

A catalogue record for this
book is available from the
National Library of Australia

'Home Education' Series

VOLUME IV.

# Ourselves: Book 2

By

Charlotte M. Mason

LIVING BOOK
**PRESS**

# 'Home Education' Series

By Charlotte M. Mason

Available from Living Book Press

---

www.LivingBookPress.com

# Preface to the 'Home Education' Series

THE educational outlook is rather misty and depressing both at home and abroad. That science should be a staple of education, that the teaching of Latin, of modern languages, of mathematics, must be reformed, that nature and handicrafts should be pressed into service for the training of the eye and hand, that boys and girls must learn to write English and therefore must know something of history and literature; and, on the other hand, that education must be made more technical and utilitarian—these, and such as these, are the cries of expedience with which we take the field. But we have no unifying principle, no definite aim; in fact, no philosophy of education. As a stream can rise no higher than its source, so it is probable that no educational effort can rise above the whole scheme of thought which gives it birth; and perhaps this is the reason of all the 'fallings from us, vanishings,' failures, and disappointments which mark our educational records.

Those of us, who have spent many years in pursuing the benign and elusive vision of Education, perceive that her approaches are regulated by a law, and that this law has yet to be evoked. We can discern its outlines, but no more. We know that it is pervasive; there is no part of a child's home-life or school-work which the law does not penetrate. It is illuminating, too, showing the value, or lack of value, of a thousand systems and expedients. It is not only a light, but a measure, providing a standard whereby all things, small and great, belonging to educational work must be tested. The law is liberal, taking in whatsoever things are true, honest, and of good report, and offering no limitation or hindrance save where excess should injure. And the path indicated by the law is continuous and progressive, with no transition stage from the cradle to the grave, except that maturity takes up the regular self-direction to which immaturity has been trained. We shall doubtless find, when we apprehend the law, that certain German thinkers— Kant, Herbart, Lotze, Froebel—are justified; that, as they say, it is 'necessary' to believe in God; that, therefore, the knowledge of God is the principal knowledge, and the chief end of education. By one more character shall we be able to recognise this perfect law of educational liberty when it shall be made evident. It has been said that 'The best idea which we can form of absolute truth is that it is able to meet every condition by which it can be tested.' This we shall expect of our law—that it shall meet every test of experiment and every test of rational investigation.

Not having received the tables of our law, we fall back upon Froebel or upon Herbart; or, if we belong to another School, upon Locke or Spencer; but we are not satisfied. A discontent, is it a divine discontent? is upon us; and assuredly we should hail a workable, effectual philosophy of education as a deliverance from much perplexity. Before this great deliverance comes to us it is probable that many tentative efforts will be put forth, having more or less of the characters of a philosophy; notably, having a central idea, a body of thought with various members working in vital harmony.

Such a theory of education, which need not be careful to call itself a system of psychology, must be in harmony with the thought movements of the age; must regard education, not as a shut-off compartment, but as being as much a part of life as birth or growth, marriage or work; and it must leave the pupil attached to the world at many points of contact. It is true that educationalists are already eager to establish such contact in several directions, but their efforts rest upon an axiom here and an idea there, and there is no broad unifying basis of thought to support the whole.

Fools rush in where angels fear to tread; and the hope that there may be many tentative efforts towards a philosophy of education, and that all of them will bring us nearer to the *magnum opus,* encourages me to launch one such attempt. The central thought, or rather body of thought, upon which I found, is the somewhat obvious fact that the child is a *person* with all the possibilities and powers included in personality. Some of the members which develop from this nucleus have been exploited from time to time by educational thinkers, and exist vaguely in the general common sense, a notion here, another there. One thesis, which is, perhaps, new, that *Education is the Science of Relations*, appears to me to solve the question of a curriculum, as showing that the object of education is to put a child in living touch with as much as may be of the life of Nature and of thought. Add to this one or two keys to self-knowledge, and the educated youth goes forth with some idea of self-management, with some pursuits, and many vital interests. My excuse for venturing to offer a solution, however tentative and passing, to the problem of education is twofold. For between thirty and forty years I have laboured without pause to establish a working and philosophic theory of education; and in the next place, each article of the educational faith I offer has been arrived at by inductive processes; and has, I think, been verified by a long and wide series of experiments. It is, however, with sincere diffidence that I venture to offer the results of this long labour; because I know that in this field there are many labourers far more able and expert than I—the 'angels' who fear to tread, so precarious is the footing!

But, if only *pour encourager les autres*, I append a short synopsis of the educational theory advanced in the volumes of the 'Home Education Series.' The treatment is not methodic, but incidental; here a little, there a little, as seemed to me most likely to meet the occasions of parents and teachers. I should add that in the course of a number of years the various essays have been prepared for the use of the Parents' Educational Union in the hope that that Society might witness for a more or less coherent body of educational thought.

> "The consequence of truth is great; therefore the judgment of it must not be negligent."
>
> WHICHCOTE.

1. Children are born *persons*.

2. They are not born either good or bad, but with possibilities for good and evil.

3. The principles of authority on the one hand and obedience on the other, are natural, necessary and fundamental; but—

4. These principles are limited by the respect due to the personality of children, which must not be encroached upon, whether by fear or love, suggestion or influence, or undue play upon any one natural desire.

5. Therefore we are limited to three educational instruments—the atmosphere of environment, the discipline of habit, and the presentation of living ideas.

6. By the saying, EDUCATION IS AN ATMO-SPHERE, it is not meant that a child should be isolated in what may be called a 'child environment,'

especially adapted and prepared; but that we should take into account the educational value of his natural home atmosphere, both as regards persons and things, and should let him live freely among his proper conditions. It stultifies a child to bring down his world to the 'child's' level.

7. By EDUCATION IS A DISCIPLINE, is meant the discipline of habits formed definitely and thoughtfully, whether habits of mind or body. Physiologists tell us of the adaptation of brain structure to habitual lines of thought—*i.e.*, to our habits.

8. In the saying that EDUCATION IS A LIFE, the need of intellectual and moral as well as of physical sustenance is implied. The mind feeds on ideas, and therefore children should have a generous curriculum.

9. But the mind is not a receptacle into which ideas must be dropped, each idea adding to an 'apperception mass' of its like, the theory upon which the Herbartian doctrine of interest rests.

10. On the contrary, a child's mind is no mere *sac* to hold ideas; but is rather, if the figure may be allowed, a spiritual *organism*, with an appetite for all knowledge. This is its proper diet, with which it is prepared to deal, and which it can digest and assimilate as the body does foodstuffs.

11. This difference is not a verbal quibble. The Herbartian doctrine lays the stress of education—the preparation of knowledge in enticing morsels, presented in due order—upon the teacher. Children

taught upon this principle are in danger of receiving much teaching with little knowledge; and the teacher's axiom is, 'What a child learns matters less than how he learns it.'

12. But, believing that the normal child has powers of mind that fit him to deal with all knowledge proper to him, we must give him a full and generous curriculum; taking care, only, that the knowledge offered to him is vital—that is, that facts are not presented without their informing ideas. Out of this conception comes the principle that,—

13. EDUCATION IS THE SCIENCE OF RELATIONS; that is, that a child has natural relations with a vast number of things and thoughts: so we must train him upon physical exercises, nature, handicrafts, science and art, and upon *many living* books; for we know that our business is, not to teach him all about anything, but to help him to make valid as many as may be of—

> 'Those first-born affinities,
>
> That fit our new existence to existing things.'

14. There are also two secrets of moral and intellectual self-management which should be offered to children; these we may call the Way of the Will and the Way of the Reason.

15. *The Way of the Will*—Children should be taught—

(*a*) To distinguish between 'I want' and 'I will.'

(*b*) That the way to will effectively is to turn our

thoughts from that which we desire but do not will.

(c) That the best way to turn our thoughts is to think of or do some quite different thing, entertaining or interesting.

(d) That, after a little rest in this way, the will returns to its work with new vigour. (This adjunct of the will is familiar to us as *diversion*, whose office it is to ease us for a time from will effort, that we may 'will' again with added power. The use of suggestion— even self-suggestion—as an aid to the will, is to be deprecated, as tending to stultify and stereotype character. It would seem that spontaneity is a condition of development, and that human nature needs the discipline of failure as well as of success).

16. *The Way of the Reason.*—We should teach children, too, not to 'lean' (too confidently) 'unto their own understanding.' because the function of reason is, to give logical demonstration (a) of mathematical truth; and (b) of an initial idea, accepted by the will. In the former case reason is, perhaps, an infallible guide, but in the second it is not always a safe one; for whether that initial idea be right or wrong, reason will confirm it by irrefragable proofs.

17. Therefore children should be taught, as they become mature enough to understand such teaching, that the chief responsibility which rests on them as persons is the acceptance or rejection of initial ideas.

To help them in this choice we should give them principles of conduct and a wide range of the knowledge fitted for them.

These three principles (15, 16 and 17) should save children from some of the loose thinking and heedless action which cause most of us to live at a lower level than we need.

18. We should allow no separation to grow up between the intellectual and 'spiritual' life of children; but should teach them that the divine Spirit has constant access to their spirits, and is their continual helper in all the interests, duties and joys of life.

*The 'Home Education' Series is so called from the title of the first volume, and not as dealing, wholly or principally, with 'Home' as opposed to 'School' education.*

# Preface

"Who was it that said 'Know thyself' came down from heaven? It is quite true-true as Gospel. It came straight to whoever said it first."—*Life of Sir Edward Burne-Jones*.

POSSIBLY we fail to give 'effective moral training based upon Christian principles' to young people because our teaching is scrappy, and rests mainly upon appeals to the emotions through tale and song. Inspiring as these are, we may not depend upon them entirely, because emotional response is short-lived, and the appeal is deadened by repetition: the response of the intellect to coherent and consecutive teaching appears, on the contrary, to be continuous and enduring. Boys and girls, youths and maidens, have as much capacity to apprehend what is presented to their minds as have their elders; and, like their elders, they take great pleasure and interest in an appeal to their understanding which discovers to them the ground-plan of human nature—a common possession.

The point of view taken in this volume is, that all beautiful and noble possibilities are present in everyone; but that each person is subject to assault and hindrance in various ways, of which he should be aware in order that he may watch and pray. Hortatory teaching is apt to bore both young people and their elders; but an ordered presentation of the possibilities that lie in human nature, and of the risks that attend these, can hardly fail to have an enlightening and stimulating effect. This volume is intended as an appeal to the young to make the most of themselves, because of the vast possibilities that are in them and of the law of God which constrains them.

The teaching in Book I. is designed for boys and girls under sixteen. That in Book II. should, perhaps, appeal to young people of any age; possibly young men and women may welcome an attempt to thrash out some of the problems which must needs perplex them. In the hands of the teachers of elementary schools, the book should give some help in the formation of character. If only half a dozen children in each such school got an idea of what is possible to them and what they should aim at, some elevation of character throughout the nation should be manifest in a single generation. In our moral as in our intellectual education, we work too entirely upon narrow utilitarian lines: we want the impulse of profounder conceptions. The middle and upper forms of a public school, and those indicated above, fairly represent the classes of readers the author has in view.

The two 'Books' are published separately in order

that each may be put into the hands of the readers
for whom it is designed; but, because parents and
teachers should make a particular study of such moral
teaching as they may offer to the young people for
whom they are responsible, it seems desirable that
the two volumes should form one of the 'Home
Education Series.' Questions are appended for the
use of more serious students. The more or less casual
ordering of young people which falls to their elders
might become more purposeful if it were laid down
upon some such carefully considered ground-plan of
human nature as this book attempts to offer. The
scheme of thought rests upon intuitive morality, as
sanctioned by the authority of Revelation.

The systems of morality formulated by authorita-
tive writers upon ethics are, perhaps, expanded a little
to include latent capacity for every kind of goodness
in all normal human beings. Some attempt has been
made to define certain limitations of reason, conscience, and the will, the disregard of which is a
fertile cause of error in human conduct.

What is sometimes described as the 'immanence
of God'; the capacity of man for relations with the
divine; and the maimed and incomplete character
of the life in which these relations are not fulfilled,
are touched upon, because these matters belong to a
knowledge which is 'the chief end of man.' The
allusions and excerpts which illustrate the text have
been carefully chosen from sources that fall within
everybody's reading, because the object is rather to

arrest the attention of the reader, and fix it, for example, upon the teaching of Scott and Plutarch, than to suggest unknown sources of edification. We are all too well content to let alone that of which we do not already know something.

AMBLESIDE, *May* 1905.

*A somewhat arbitrary use has been made of certain terms— 'daemon,' for example—when such use appeared to lend itself to clearness or force in putting the case.*

# Contents

# CHAPTER IV

### THE RULINGS OF CONSCIENCE IN THE HOUSE OF BODY: CHASTITY (*Part I.*)

# CHAPTER V

### THE RULINGS OF CONSCIENCE IN THE HOUSE OF BODY: CHASTITY (*Part II.*)

#### *Ordered Friendship*

# CHAPTER VI

### THE RULINGS OF CONSCIENCE IN THE HOUSE OF BODY: CHASTITY (PART III.)

# CHAPTER VII

### THE RULINGS OF CONSCIENCE IN THE HOUSE OF BODY: FORTITUDE

# CHAPTER VIII

### THE RULINGS OF CONSCIENCE IN THE HOUSE OF BODY: PRUDENCE

## SECTION II.—CONSCIENCE IN THE HOUSE OF MIND

### CHAPTER IX

#### OPINIONS 'IN THE AIR'

### CHAPTER X

#### THE UNINSTRUCTED CONSCIENCE

### CHAPTER XI

#### THE INSTRUCTED CONSCIENCE

### CHAPTER XII

#### SOME INSTRUCTIONS OF CONSCIENCE: POETRY, NOVELS, ESSAYS

### CHAPTER XIII

#### SOME INSTRUCTIONS OF CONSCIENCE: HISTORY AND PHILOSOPHY

### CHAPTER XIV

#### SOME INSTRUCTIONS OF CONSCIENCE: THEOLOGY

Theology-The divine method—The Bible contains a revelation
of God—The higher criticism—Indecision—Study of the
Bible—'Revelation' of the Bible unique—No revelation

## CHAPTER XV

### SOME INSTRUCTIONS OF CONSCIENCE: NATURE SCIENCE, ART

## CHAPTER XVI

### SOME INSTRUCTIONS OF CONSCIENCE: SOCIOLOGY SELF-KNOWLEDGE

## SECTION III.-THE FUNCTION OF CONSCIENCE

## CHAPTER XVII

### CONVICTION OF SIN

## CHAPTER XVIII

### TEMPTATION

## CHAPTER XIX

### DUTY AND LAW

# PART II

# THE WILL

## CHAPTER I

### THE WILL-LESS LIFE

## CHAPTER II

### WILL AND WILFULNESS

## CHAPTER III

### WILL NOT MORAL OR IMMORAL

## CHAPTER IV

### THE WILL AND ITS PEERS

## CHAPTER V

### The Function of Will

## CHAPTER VI

### The Scope of Will

## CHAPTER VII

### Self-Control—Self-Restraint—Self-Command—Self-Denial

## CHAPTER VIII

### The Effort of Decision

## CHAPTER IX

### Intention—Purpose—Resolutions

## CHAPTER X

### A Way of the Will

## CHAPTER XI

### FREEWILL

## PART III

## THE SOUL

## CHAPTER I

### THE CAPACITIES OF THE SOUL

## CHAPTER II

### THE DISABILITIES OF THE SOUL

## CHAPTER III

### THE KNOWLEDGE OF GOD

## CHAPTER IV

### PRAYER

## CHAPTER V

### THANKSGIVING

## CHAPTER VI

### PRAISE

## CHAPTER VII

### FAITH IN GOD

## APPENDIX

### QUESTIONS FOR THE USE OF STUDENTS

## INDEX

# Ourselves

## Book II.—Self-Direction

# Ourselves

# Book II.—Self-Direction

"Order my goings."

## INTRODUCTORY

IN Book I. of *Ourselves*, which deals with Self-knowledge, I have tried to lay before the reader a pano-
ramic view of the Kingdom of Mansoul. I shall
continue to use the expression, Mansoul, which we
owe to Bunyan, because I do not know any other that
suggests a view from the outside, as if one surveyed
a tract of country from an eminence. From our
imaginary height, we have—supposing that the reader
has been my fellow-student in the considerations that
occupied the former volume—taken a bird's-eye view
of the riches of Mansoul, of the wonderful capacities
there are in every human being to enter upon the
world as a great inheritance.

All its beauty and all its thought are open to everyone; everyone may take service for the world's uses;
everyone may climb those delectable mountains in the
recesses of his own nature from whence he gets the

1

vision of the city of God. If Mansoul has infinite
resources and glorious possibilities, it has also perils,
any one of which may bring devastation and ruin.
None of these perils is inevitable, because Mansoul
is a kingdom under an established government. It
is convenient to think of this government as carried
on in four Chambers.

The House of Body is, we have seen, sustained by
the Appetites; but ruined when any one of these
appetites obtains sole control. The five Senses are,
as it were, pages running between body and mind,
and ministering to both.

The House of Mind is amazingly ordered with a
view to the getting of knowledge. "Studies serve
for delight, for ornament, and for ability," is writ large
upon the portals, and within are the powers fitted to
deal with all knowledge. There is Intellect, waiting
to apprehend knowledge of many sorts; Imagination,
taking impressions, living pictures of the glories of the
past and the behaviour of the remote; there is the
Aesthetic Sense, whose motto is, "A thing of beauty
is a joy for ever," ready to appropriate every thing
of beauty, whether picture, poem, wind-flower, or
starry heavens—a possession of joy for ever. Reason
is there, eager to discern causes and consequences, to
know the why and the wherefore of every fact that
comes before the mind; and lest, with all these powers,
Mind should become an uninhabited house, with rusty
hinges and cobwebbed panes, there are certain Desires
which bestir us to feed the mind, in much the same
way as our Appetites clamour for the food of the
body.

Just as each Appetite carries in itself the possibilities
of excess and universal ruin to Mansoul, so each of

these admirable functions of the mind has what we have called its daemons; and each of these may not only paralyse that mind-power which it shadows, but may distort and enfeeble the whole of the powers of Mind.

The House of Heart is, we have seen, dominated, in every Mansoul, by two benign powers, Love and Justice. Pity, Benevolence, Sympathy, Kindness, Generosity, Gratitude, Courage, Loyalty, Humility, Gladness, are among the lords in waiting attendant upon Love; and Justice has its own attendant virtues—Gentleness, Courtesy, Candour, Respect, Discernment, Appreciation, Veracity, Integrity, and more.

Temperance, Soberness, and Chastity, too, are of the household of Justice; for these include that justice which we owe to ourselves; but, alas! Upon every one of these waits its appropriate daemon, and the safe-conduct of life depends, first, upon discerning, and then upon avoiding, the malevolent dispositions which are ready to devastate the House of Heart. We know how Cowardice, Meanness, Rudeness, Calumny, Envy, and a hundred other powers of evil beset us. The perils are so great, the risks so numerous, that many a goodly Mansoul perishes with out ever realising the vast wealth which belongs to it—like a prince brought up in peasant's estate, and unaware of his birthright. Those who begin to realise how much is possible to Mansoul, and how many are the perils of the way, know that a certain duty of self-direction belongs to them; and that powers for this direction are lodged in them as truly as are intellect and imagination, hunger and thirst.

The governing powers lodged within us are the

Conscience and the Will; but conscience (even the conscience of a good Christian person) is not capable of judging for us, in the various affairs of our life, without instruction, any more than the intellect of the ignorant mind can pronounce upon a problem of the differential calculus.

Therefore, Conscience must learn its lessons, regular and progressive lessons, upon the affairs of body, heart, and mind. One of the objects of this volume is to point out some of the courses of instruction proper for conscience, and some of the ends at which this instruction should aim. The affairs of the heart are so far interdependent with those of mind and body that the separate consideration we need give them at present is contained in the former volume of *Ourselves*.

Concerning the Will, too, the highest but one of all the powers of Mansoul, we need instruction. Persons commonly suppose that the action of the will is automatic; but no power of Mansoul acts by itself and of itself; and some little study of the 'way of the will'—which has the ordering of every other power—may help us to understand the functions of what we have called the prime minister in the kingdom of Mansoul.

It is well, too, that we should know something of the Soul, the name we give to that within us which has capacity for the knowledge and love of God, for prayer and praise and faith, for the enthronement of the King, whose right it is to reign over Mansoul. We may believe that the Creator is honoured by our attempt to know something of the powers and the perils belonging to that human nature with which He has endowed us.

# PART I

# CONSCIENCE

## *CONSCIENCE IN THE HOUSE OF BODY*

### CHAPTER I

#### THE COURT OF APPEAL

**Conscience, the Judge, always in Court.—**
The affairs of Mansoul do not by any means go
right of themselves. We have seen how the powers
that be, in body, mind, and heart, are in conflict
with one another, each of them trying for sole rule
in Mansoul; and again, how the best servants of
the state are beset by certain daemons. But all
this conflict and rivalry is provided against. There
is a Court of Appeal always open, and therein sits
the Lord Chief Justice whom we call Conscience.
Let us consider for a moment what is the office of
a judge in a court of law. He does not know, and
is not expected to know, the rights and wrongs of
every case brought before him. Advocates on both
sides get up these and set them in order before the
judge; but he is in authority; he knows the law,
and gives the right decision upon what he knows.

**Everyone has a Sense of Duty.**—Just so, with Conscience. He proclaims the law, that is, Duty. No Mansoul is left without the sense of *ought*— everyone knows that certain behaviour is *due* from him, that he *owes* the ordering of his conduct to a higher Power. *Duty*, that which is *due* from us; *ought*, that which we *owe*, is the proclamation of Conscience. We are not our own; but God, who has given us life, and whose we are, has planted within us Conscience, to remind us continually that we owe ourselves to Him, and must order our ways to please Him, and that He is the Judge who will visit every offence surely and directly, if not to-day, then to-morrow. Conscience informs us, too, of the reason of this judging of our God. Judging is saving. It is the continual calling of us back from wrong ways, which injure and ruin, into right ways of peace and happiness. All this Conscience testifies to us; morning by morning, hour by hour, he witnesses that we are not free to do what we like, but must do what we ought.

**Conscience may give Wrong Judgments.**— But if Conscience gives judgment in every Man-soul, how is it that people continually go wrong? As we have seen, there is apt to be anarchy in the State. Sloth or temper, pride or envy, betrays Mansoul.

I need not dwell upon the fate of those who will not listen to Conscience; but there is danger, too, for those who do listen. We hear it said that a man acts 'up to his lights,' or 'according to his lights.' However wrong he may be, there are some who excuse him because he knew no better. If the man has had no chance of knowing better, the excuse may be allowed; but it is not enough to act according to our lights, if we *choose* to carry a dim wick in a dirty lantern, when we might have a good light

**Conscience may be tampered with.**—We have seen that the judge is not familiar with the ins and outs of the case he tries. It is so with the judge of our bosom. He, too, listens to advocates; Inclination hires Reason to plead before Conscience; and Reason is so subtle and convincing that the judge gives the verdict for the defendant. 'Obey the law,' says Conscience; but, 'This that I choose to do is the law,' says Reason, on behalf of the defendant. 'Then, defendant' (*i.e.* Inclination), 'you may do the thing you choose.' This subtle misleading of Conscience is an art practised alike by little children and hardened criminals. It is possible that in this sense everyone acts up to his lights; he justifies himself; his reason proves that what he does is right in the circumstances, and Conscience lets him off—never ceasing to cry, 'Thou shalt do right,' but leaving each one free, to some extent, to decide as to what is right.

It is well we should know this limit to the power of Conscience, for many reasons; amongst others, it helps us to understand the histories of nations and individuals.

**Conscience must be instructed.**—It is necessary that we should all know something about the constitution of Mansoul, in order that we may recognise the voice of the speaker who instructs reason to put the case to conscience. Envy, for example, does not say, 'I hate Jones because he has a rich father,' or, 'because he scores, whether in lessons or games,' or 'because he is popular with the other fellows.' Envy pretends that all he wishes for is fair play. 'It's not fair that one fellow should have lots of pocket-money and another have to pinch and scrape.' 'Jones got up by a fluke in the Ovid.' 'He's always hunting for popularity: no decent fellow would lay himself out like that' With arguments such as these does envy prompt reason, who makes out a good case before conscience, and the defendant gets off.

But the person who knows that any depreciation of another, by way of making much of ourselves, comes of envy, and not justice, is on his guard. He keeps his tongue from evil and his thoughts from malice, and submits to the condemnation of his unbiased conscience.

This straight way of looking at things is what our Lord calls the single eye. Many people seem to have it by nature, and cannot easily be deceived into calling wrong, right. But evil is specious and ready; and it is well for each of us to take pains that we may recognise misrepresentations brought before conscience. An instructed conscience rarely makes mistakes.

# CHAPTER II

## THE INSTRUCTION OF CONSCIENCE

**Instruction by Books.**—The instructed conscience knows that Temperance, Chastity, Fortitude, Prudence must rule in the House of Body. But how is the conscience to become instructed? Life brings us many lessons: when we see others do well, conscience approves and learns; when others do ill, conscience condemns. But we want a wider range of knowledge than the life about us affords, and books are our best teachers.

There is no nice shade of conduct which is not described or exemplified in the vast treasure-house of literature. History and biography are full of instruction in righteousness; but what is properly called literature, that is, poetry, essays, the drama, and novels, is perhaps the most useful for our moral instruction, because the authors bring their insight to bear in a way they would hesitate to employ when writing about actual persons. Autobiographies, again, often lift the veil, for the writer may make free with himself. In the Bible the lives of men and the history of a nation are told without the reticence which authors are apt to use in telling of the offences of the good or the vices of the bad.

Plutarch, perhaps alone among biographers, writes with comparable candour, if not always with equal justice.

**The Poet and the Essayist are our Teachers.** —A child gets moral notions from the fairy-tales he delights in, as do his elders from tale and verse. So nice a critic as Matthew Arnold tells us that poetry is a criticism of life; so it is, both a criticism and an inspiration; and most of us carry in our minds tags of verse which shape our conduct more than we know;—

> "Wisdom is ofttimes nearer when we stoop
> Than when we soar."[1]

> "The friends thou hast, and their adoption tried,
> Grapple them to thy soul with hooks of steel."[2]

A thousand thoughts that burn come to us on the wings of verse; and, conceive how our lives would be impoverished were we to awake one day and find that the Psalms had disappeared from the world and from the thoughts of men! Proverbs, too, the words of the wise king and the sayings of the common folk, come to us as if they were auguries; while the essayists deal with conduct and give much delicate instruction, which reaches us the more surely through the charm of their style.

**So are the Novelists and the Dramatists.—** Perhaps the dramatists and novelists have done the most for our teaching; but not the works of every playwright and novelist are good 'for example of life and instruction in manners.' We are safest with those which have lived long enough to become classics; and this, for two reasons. The fact that

---

[1] Wordsworth.      [2] *Hamlet.*

they have not been allowed to die proves in itself that the authors have that to say, and a way of saying it, which the world cannot do without. In the next place, the older novels and plays deal with conduct, and conduct is our chief concern in life. Modern works of the kind deal largely with emotions, a less wholesome subject of contemplation. Having found the book which has a message for us, let us not be guilty of the folly of saying we *have read* it. We might as well say we have breakfasted, as if breakfasting on one day should last us for every day! The book that helps us deserves many readings, for assimilation comes by slow degrees.

Literature is full of teaching, by precept and example, concerning the management of our physical nature. I shall offer a lesson here and there by way of sample, but no doubt the reader will think of many better teachings; and that is as it should be; the way such teaching should come to us is, here a little and there a little, incidentally, from books which we read for the interest of the story, the beauty of the poem, or the grace of the writing.

# CHAPTER III

## THE RULINGS OF CONSCIENCE IN THE HOUSE
## OF BODY: TEMPERANCE

**Temperance in Eating.**—Who can forget how 'the fortunes of Nigel' turned upon that mess which Laurie Linklater prepared after the King's own heart? The telling is humorous; but not all the King's scholarship enables us to get over the supping of the cock-a-leekie! Thus Scott prepares us:—"But nobody among these brave English cooks can kittle up his Majesty's most sacred palate with our own gusty Scotch dishes. So I e'en betook myself to my craft and concocted a mess of friar's chicken for the soup, and a savoury hachis, that made the whole cabal coup the crans; and, instead of disgrace, I came by preferment." It was through these same gusty Scotch dishes that James was approached, and Laurie Linklater figures as a *deus ex machina*. Richie Moniplies "having reached the palace in safety demanded to see Master Linklater, the under-clerk of his Majesty's kitchen. The reply was that he was not to be spoken withal, being then employed in cooking a mess of cock-a-leekie for the King's own mouth. 'Tell him,' said Moniplies, 'that it is a dear countryman of his, who seeks to converse with him on matter of high import . . . I maun speak with the King.' 'The King? Ye are red wud,' said Link later . . . . 'I will have neither hand nor foot in the matter,' said the cautious clerk of the kitchen; 'but there is his Majesty's mess of cock-a-leekie just going to be served to him in his closet—I cannot prevent you from putting the letter between the gilt-bowl and the platter; his sacred Majesty will see it when he lifts the bowl, for he aye drinks out the broth.'"

And *The Fortunes of Nigel* closes with the King's last word—"And, my lords and lieges, let us all to our dinner, for the cock-a-leekie is cooling."[1]

Where's the harm? In this: King James's moral worth and intelligence are swamped, his dignity of character and title to respect forfeited, through igno-minious failures in self-restraint in this and other matters. Did not the patriarch Isaac, too, lend himself to the deception which divided his family by his love for that savoury meat upon which so much turns? It is well and a sign of health that we should like and enjoy our 'meat,' but to love and long for any par-ticular dish is of the nature of intemperance. So thought Plutarch when he tells us this tale[2] of his bringing up:—

"Our master (says he) having one day observed that we had indulged ourselves too luxuriously at dinner, at his afternoon lecture ordered his freedman to give his own son the discipline of the whip in our presence; signifying at the same time that he suffered this punishment because he could not eat his victuals without sauce. The philosopher all the

---

[1] *The Fortunes of Nigel*, by Sir Walter Scott
[2] Preface to Plutarch's *Lives*.

while had his eye upon us, and we knew well for whom this example of punishment was intended."

**In Drinking.**—That Le Balafre[1] should behave like a sot is what we expect of his lower nature; but it is painful that the generous and noble Lord Crawford should lose dignity and self-possession over the wine-cup. The occasion is the banquet given by the Mess to welcome the election of Quentin Durward. "At present, however, Lord Crawford declined occupying the seat prepared for him, and bidding them 'hold themselves merry,' stood looking on at the revel with a countenance which seemed greatly to enjoy it. 'Let him alone,' whispered Cunningham to Lindesay, as the latter offered wine to their noble Captain, 'let him alone—hurry no man's cattle—let him take it of his own accord.' In fact, the old Lord, who at first smiled, shook his head, and placed the untasted wine-cup before him, began presently, as if it were in absence of mind, to sip a little of the contents, and in doing so, fortunately recollected that it would be ill luck did he not drink a draught to the health of the gallant lad who had joined them this day. . . . The good old Lord could not but in courtesy do reason to this pledge also, and gliding into the ready chair, as it were, without reflecting what he was doing he caused Quentin to come up beside him, and assailed him with many more questions concerning the state of Scotland, and the great families there, than he was well able to answer; while ever and anon, in the course of his queries, the good Lord kissed the wine-cup by way of parenthesis, remarking that sociality became Scottish gentlemen, but that young men, like Quentin, ought to practise

[1] *Quentin Durwald*, by Sir Walter Scott.

it cautiously, lest it might degenerate into excess; upon which occasion he uttered many excellent things, until his own tongue, although employed in the praises of temperance, began to articulate something thicker than usual."

Times have changed since Quentin Durward played his part; and if men still drink, they are commonly not men of Lord Crawford's dignity of character. People begin to see that plain living and high thinking go together; self-restraint is practised both in eating and drinking, and the day is coming when excess in either will be regarded with general contempt.

**In taking our Ease.**—Miss Edgeworth's *Lazy Lawrence* has passed into a proverb; and many a more attractive hero is tarred with the same brush. Here is Harry Warrington, for example:—

"Harry's lace and linen were as fine as his aunt could desire. He purchased the shaving-plate of the toyshop women, and a couple of magnificent brocade bedgowns, in which his worship lolled at ease and sipped his chocolate of a morning. He had swords and walking-canes and French watches with painted backs and diamond settings, and snuff-boxes enamelled by artists of the same cunning nation. He had a levee of grooms, jockeys, tradesmen, daily waiting in his ante-room, and admitted one by one to him, and Parson Sampson, over his chocolate, by Gumbo, the groom of the chambers. We have no account of the men whom Mr Gumbo had now under him. Certain it is that no single negro could have taken care of all the fine things which Mr Warrington now possessed, let alone the horses and the post-chaise which his honour had bought. Also Harry instructed himself in the arts which became a gentleman in those days. A French fencing-master, and a dancing-master of the same nation, resided at Tunbridge during that season when Harry made his appearance: these men of science the young Virginian sedulously frequented, and acquired considerable skill and grace in the peaceful and warlike accomplishments which they taught. Ere many weeks were over he could handle the foils against his master or any frequenter of the fencing-school. . . . As for riding, though Mr Warrington took a few lessons on the great horse from a riding-master who came to Tunbridge, he declared that their own Virginian manner was well enough for him."[1]

Here we have the pursuits of busy idleness; for idleness is generally busy: Hogarth painted what Thackeray describes, this same luxury and *abandon* of idleness. Such another idler was Charles II.; while he was a great walker, he shirked every hint of the work proper to his condition. But history and fiction, and, alas, everyday life, afford many examples of men and women who never bestir themselves to catch the flying opportunity.

**In Day-Dreaming.**—There are other kinds of intemperance besides the grosser sorts of over-eating, over-drinking, over sleeping. Nathaniel Hawthorne[2] describes another type of idleness in Hepzibah Pyncheon, the solitary old maid who inhabited the House of the Seven Gables, and spent her days in the erection of curious castles in the air.

"All the while Hepzibah was perfecting the scheme of her little shop, she had cherished an unacknowledged idea that some harlequin trick

[1] *The Virginians*, by W. M. Thackeray.
[2] *The House of the Seven Gables.*

of fortune would intervene in her favour. For example, an uncle—who had sailed for India fifty years before, and had never been heard of since—might yet return, and adopt her to be the comfort of his very extreme and decrepit age, and adorn her with pearls, diamonds, oriental shawls, and turbans, and make her the ultimate heiress of his unreckonable riches. Or the member of parliament, now at the head of the English branch of the family,—with which the elder stock, on this side of the Atlantic, had held little or no intercourse for the last two centuries,—this eminent gentleman might invite Hepzibah to quit the ruinous House of the Seven Gables, and come over to dwell with her kindred at Pyncheon Hall . . . . But, for reasons the most imperative, she could not yield to his request."

But, indeed, there is little to be said for the slothful:—

> How comes it that of all
> The lusts that could enthral
> Yon Bible worthies to so hapless fall,
> Sloth shows not first,
> Hell-frame acurst,
> Where every pestilent root of ill is nursed?
> Who slips must erst have stood,
> Have made his foothold good,
> Have risen and held him up, ere fall he could:
> But who lies prone,
> Such toils unknown,
> May comfort him, lapse for him is there none;
> The sum of ill-doing is—leaving undone.

**'Know thy Work and do it.'**—Let us hear Carlyle,[1] the apostle of work, upon idleness and work:—"And who art thou that braggest of thy

[1] *Past and Present.*

life of Idleness; complacently showest thy bright gilt equipages; sumptuous cushions; appliances for folding of the hands to mere sleep? . . . One monster there is in the world: the idle man. . . . The latest gospel in this world is, Know thy work and do it: . . . know what thou canst work at; and work at it, like a Hercules! That will be thy better plan.

"It has been written, 'An endless significance lies in work'; a man perfects himself by working. Foul jungles are cleared away, fair seed-fields rise instead, and stately cities; and withal the man himself first ceases to be a jungle and foul unwholesome desert thereby. The man is now a man."

**Principle underlying Temperance.**—Conscience is not, in fact, so much concerned with the manner of our intemperance as with the underlying principle which St Paul sets forth when he condemns those who "worship and serve the creature more than the Creator." This is the principle according to which we shall be justified or condemned; and, in its light, we have reason to be suspicious of any system of diet or exercise which bespeaks *excessive* concern for the body, whether that concern be shown by a diet of nuts and apples, of peacocks' brains, or of cock-a-leekie. England is in serious danger of giving herself over to the worship of a deity whom we all honour as *Hygeia*. But never did men bow down before so elusive a goddess, for the more she is pursued, the more she flees; while she is ready with smiles and favours for him who never casts a thought her way. In truth and sober earnest, the pursuit of physical (and mental) well-being is taking its place amongst us as a religious cult; and the danger of such a cult is, lest we concentrate our minds, not upon Christ, but upon our own consciousness. We 'have faith' to produce in ourselves certain comfortable attitudes of mind and body; this serenity satisfies us, and we forget the danger of exalting the concerns of the creature above the worship of the Creator. The essence of Christianity is passionate love and loyalty towards a divine Person: and faith, the adoring regard of the soul, must needs make us like Him who is 'meek and lowly of heart.' A faith which raises us to a 'higher plane' should be suspect of the Christian conscience, as seeking to serve ourselves of the power of Christ, less to His glory than our own satisfaction.

Well said Carlyle that, whether you or I be in a state of well-being or not 'is not the central fact of the Universe.'

If undue attention to the physical nature be a kind of intemperance, still more so is the neglect of that nature through which every function we are enabled for is performed; and such neglect has its sources in the indifference of sloth and the excesses of greed. '*Take no thought* for the life, what ye shall eat or what ye shall drink.' 'Eat that which is set before you.' These are the rules laid down by our Master, whereby we may 'keep our bodies in temperance, soberness, and chastity.' 'Take no thought,' for all offences against the body begin in the thoughts.

**We Live in our Times.**—I appear to have wandered wide of the mark, seeing that my subject is the dealings of Conscience with the House of Body in the matter of Temperance; but, indeed, it is necessary to keep a wide outlook upon the movements of the day, as well as upon those of our own appetites. We live with our times; and we must bear in mind that there is no freak of the moment,—whether it be that fruit-eating colony in the Pacific, or the living upon one meal a day, or the not permitting ourselves to drink anything at all, not even water,—for which Reason is not capable of being enlisted as special pleader. Only the instructed conscience is proof against persuasion. Let us hail *Punch* as our faithful mentor; whether we would be quadrumanous persons or nut-eaters, *Punch* laughs us into common sense!

# CHAPTER IV

## THE RULINGS OF CONSCIENCE IN THE HOUSE
## OF BODY: CHASTITY

**Chastity of Soul.**—In this field, also, the instructed Conscience takes a wide survey. The law forbids all sins of impurity, whether in imagination, word, or deed: of this we are aware, but do we recognise that the proportion of Love must be preserved as duly as the proportion of Faith? The instructed Conscience learns to regard all excessive affection, undue fondness, as sullying the chastity of the self-controlled soul. Any friendship, even if it be friendship between mother and child, which is over-fond and exclusive, making the one continually necessary to the other, and shutting out other claims of duty and affection, is suspect of the clear Conscience. To be 'all in all to each other' is not a quite pure desire, apart from the question of sex; for the chaste soul is, after the manner of Giotto's picture, walled within a tower. *Noli me tangere* is the law it chooses to obey, to the exclusion of all too close intimacies.

**The Tragedy of 'Edward II.'**[1]—Perhaps nowhere is this law of the pure life more plainly indicated—by breach—than in the most sorrowful

[1] Marlowe.

21

tragedy of *Edward II.*, as set forth by Christopher Marlowe. Let us see how the tale goes, for one such lesson of life is worth many counsels and innumerable resolutions. Excess in affection is a weakness that besets generous natures, and King Edward is generous:—

> "My father is deceased! Come, Gaveston,
> And share the kingdom with thy dearest friend"

Here indeed is friendship! Eager to share all fortune to the utmost with a friend. And Gaveston is ready with love for love—

> "Sweet prince, I come; these, these thy amorous lines
> Might have enforced me to have swum from France."

The fond friendship is resented by the nobles, who have their own claims upon the King. They call a council and remonstrate, adding prayers and threats of rebellion. The King concludes the meeting with—

> "I'll either die or live with Gaveston."
> *Gaveston.* "I can no longer keep me from my lord."
>
> *Edward.* "What, Gaveston! welcome!—kiss not my hand—
> Embrace me, Gaveston, as I do thee.
> Why should'st thou kneel? know'st thou not who I am?
> Thy friend, thyself, another Gaveston!"

Edward pours titles, lands, and honours upon his friend with a free hand; nay, gives him his very seal—

> "Save or condemn, and in our name command
> Whatso thy mind affects, or fancy likes."

Again the nobles and great churchmen hold council as to how to dispose of 'that peevish Frenchman,'— happy phrase, for the favourite or fondly beloved friend is ever peevish, ready to take offence, quick to resent.

"Thus arm in arm the King and he doth march,"
says Lancaster; and Warwick adds, "Thus leaning
on the shoulder of the King he nods and scorns and
smiles at those that pass."

The Queen herself complains,—

> "For now, my lord, the King regards me not,
> But doats upon the love of Gaveston.
> He claps his cheek, and hangs about his neck,
> Smiles in his face, and whispers in his ears;
> And when I comes he frowns, as who should say,
> 'Go whither thou wilt, seeing I have Gaveston.'"

The barons compass the exile of the favourite, and
the King cries,—

> "And long thou shalt not stay, or if thou dost,
> I'll come to thee; my love shall ne'er decline."

They exchange pictures, and Edward says,—

> "Here take my picture and let me wear thine;
> O, might I keep thee here as I do this,
> Happy were I! but now most miserable!
>
> Kind words and mutual talk makes our grief greater:
> Therefore, with dumb embracement, let us part—
> Stay, Gaveston, I cannot leave thee thus."

Edward's threats and blandishments move Isabella;
she, through the younger Mortimer, works upon the
nobles, and Gaveston is recalled from his short exile
in Ireland. The Queen brings the news to her lord,
and is rewarded with momentary affection; Edward,
in his elation, distributes rewards and praises amongst
his nobles.

But the favourite, on his return, is as intolerable as
ever, and the barons as intolerant. The King lives
only in his 'minion,' and himself prepares for civil war,
to 'abate these barons' pride.' One more attempt

the barons make to convince the King of the ruin to the State brought about by his absorption in his favourite. The gifts and triumphs, masques and shows, bestowed on Gaveston have drained the treasury; rebellion threatens, deposition must follow; the King's garrisons are beaten out of France; the wild 'Oneyl' is making himself master of Ireland; the Scots make unresisted inroads in the north, the Dane commands the narrow seas;—

> "What foreign prince sends thee ambassadors?"
> "Thy gentle queen, sole sister to Valois,
>   Complains that thou hast left her all forlorn."

The peers no longer attend the royal court. The people make ballads and rhymes of scorn.

Is the King moved? Not he. The remonstrances of the barons make them traitors in his eyes, and all the result is,—

> "Poor Gaveston, that he has no friend but me!
> Do what they can, we'll live in Tynemouth here,
> And, so I walk with him about the walls,
> What care I though the Earls begirt us round? "

Things go from bad to worse, till, in the end, the exasperated barons behead Gaveston. But is the kingdom to have release from the intolerable yoke it has borne? No; for the news of the former favourite's death had not yet staled, when,—

> "And in this place of honour and of trust,
> Spencer, sweet Spencer, I adopt thee here."

Spencer, too, had loved Gaveston; but the King only follows the rule. Our fond and absorbing friendships are succeeded by others as fond and absorbing, not precisely out of fickleness, but because the enervated, emasculated nature can no longer exist without the sweet philanderings to which it has accustomed itself.

The tragical tale continues through rebellion, insurrection, and civil war; the one gleam of brightness being the young Prince Edward, who believes in his father through good report and ill,—

> "I warrant you, I'll win his highness quickly;
> 'A loves me better than a thousand Spencers."

And the King, when he learns how his wife dishonours him, his people desert him, he, too, has a thought for his child,—

> "Ah, nothing grieves me, but my little boy
> Is thus misled to countenance their ills."

All goes on as before. Spencer, by Isabella's order, is arrested in the presence of the King:—

> "Spencer, ah! sweet Spencer, thus then must we part."
> *Spencer.* "Oh! is he gone? Is noble Edward gone?
> Parted from hence? Never to see us more?"—

for there seems to be no doubt that his friends gave love for love to the over-fond monarch.

The successive imprisonments follow; then, the final message:—

> "Commend me to my son, and bid him rule
> Better than I. Yet how have I transgressed,
> Unless it be with too much clemency?"

**Each of us, King in his own Realm.**—We need not follow the tragedy to the end; but this note—"Yet how have I transgressed?"—is full of profound instruction. His own ruined life, his devastated kingdom, dishonoured wife, loyal subjects converted into traitors and assassins—all these lay at the door of the King; and he asks at the end, "Yet how have I transgressed?" His uninstructed

Conscience threw no light upon the fatal error of his life. He *chose* those duties which he would fulfil; and his code would appear to contain but one commandment,—'Be faithful to thy friend.' Never once did it dawn upon him that we may not choose amongst our duties, or that a self-elected duty may become a vice. You say, 'Ah, yes, if you are a a king; but happily lesser people are free to please themselves.' Indeed we are not. Each of us stands king amongst a thousand relations, duties, interests, proper to us. If we choose to yield ourselves to the domination of another, so that our will is paralysed and we are unable to think or act except upon that other's initiative, are incapable of being happy and at ease except in his presence, then we too have sown disorder in a realm, less wide and great than that of the unhappy Edward, but our own realm, for which *we* are responsible.

**We are not Free to give Ourselves without Reserve.**—Men seem, on the whole, to have learnt restraint in their friendships since the Tudor days when Marlowe thought it well to offer this lesson to the world, perhaps because in his day men admired men with such fond and passionate intensity. But this is not strictly a question of sex; schoolboy and schoolboy, girl and girl, man and woman, and woman and woman, there are, for whom life means no more than this manner of doting fondness for the beloved object. This is the sort of thing:—

"'Our *pension* was full of mystery and romance,' said Coquette, brightening up,' because of two German young ladies who were there. They introduced— what shall I call it?—exaltation. Do you know what it is? When one girl makes another *exaltee*, because of her goodness or her beauty, and worships her, and kisses her dress when she passes her, and serves her in all things, yet does not speak to her. And the girl who is *exaltee*—she must be proud and cold, and show scorn for her attendant—even although she has been her friend. It was these German young ladies from the Bohemian Wald who introduced it—and they were tall and dark, and very beautiful, and many would have wished to make them *exaltees*, but they were always the first to seek out someone whom they admired very much, and no one was so humble and obedient as they were. All the pension was filled with it—it was a religion, an enthusiasm—and you would see girls crying and kneeling on the floor, to show their love and admiration for their friend.'"[1]

Plutarch[2] of course, knows all about this matter. "He (Agesilaus) had a private and more sensible cause of uneasiness in his attachment to the son of Spithridates; though, while he was with him, he had made a point to combat that attachment. One day Megabates approached to salute him, and Agesilaus declined that mark of his affection. The youth after this was more distant in his addresses. Then Agesilaus was sorry for the repulse he had given him, and pretended to wonder why Megabates kept at such a distance. His friends told him he must blame himself for rejecting his former application. 'He would still,' said they, 'be glad to pay his most obliging respects to you; but take care you do not reject them again.' Agesilaus was silent for some time; and when he had considered the thing, he said, 'Do not mention it to him, for this second victory

---

[1] *A Daughter of Heth*, by William Black.
[2] *Life of Agesilaus.*

over myself gives me more pleasure than I should have in turning all I look upon to gold.'"

So great an affection, doubtless, argues a generous Heart; but that is not enough; a magnanimous Mind and an instructed Conscience must go to the preservation of the soul's chastity. We are not our own to give ourselves away without reserve.

# CHAPTER V

## THE RULINGS OF CONSCIENCE IN THE HOUSE
## OF BODY: CHASTITY (*Part II.*)

*Ordered Friendship*

**A Sane and Generous Friendship.**—But there
are a thousand records of temperate, wholesome, and
noble friendships for one of feeble excess. The
classic friendships are too well known to be quoted.
But here is a companionship of a healthy kind:—

"Are you not my only friend? and have you not
acquired a right to share my wealth? Answer
me that, Alan Fairford. When I was brought from
the solitude of my mother's dwelling into the tumult
of the Gaits' class at the High School—when I was
mocked for my English accent—salted with snow as
a Southern—rolled in the gutter for a Saxon pock-
pudding,—who with stout arguments, and stouter
blows, stood forth my defender?—Why, Alan Fairford. Who beat me soundly when I brought the
arrogance of an only son, and of course, a spoilt
urchin, to the forms of the little republic?—Why,
Alan . . . . You taught me to keep my fingers off the
weak, and to clench my fist against the strong—to
carry no tales out of school—to stand forth like a
true man—obey the stern order of a *Pande manum,*

and endure my pawmies without wincing, like one that is determined not to be the better for them. In a word, before I knew thee I knew nothing. At college it was the same. When I was incorrigibly idle, your example and encouragement roused me to mental exertion and showed me the way to intellectual enjoyment. You made me an historian, a metaphysician (*invita Minerva*)—nay, by Heaven! You had almost made an advocate of me, as well as of yourself."[1]

Though a temperate friendship, that between Alan Fairford and Darsie Latimer was no alliance of the loose, commonplace sort. Friendship was subordinated to duty while things went well. Alan prepared earnestly for his career, and was a dutiful and affectionate son to a rather exacting father. But when his friend is in danger, this canny Alan throws up his chances and endangers his life with uncalculating ardour. The young advocate has made his first appearance with marked success in a difficult case. He is carrying the court with him when the strip of paper reaches him which tells of Darsie's danger. "He stopped short in his harangue—gazed on the paper with a look of surprise and horror—uttered an exclamation, and flinging down the brief which he had in his hand, hurried out of court without returning a single word of answer to the various questions, 'What was the matter?'—'Was he taken unwell?' —'Should not a chair be called?' etc., etc." He leaves the following lines for his father: "You will not, I trust, be surprised, nor perhaps very much displeased, to learn that I am on my way to Dumfriesshire, to learn, by my own personal investigation, the present state of my dear friend, and afford him

[1] *Redgauntlet*, by Sir Walter Scott.

such relief as may be in my power, and which, I trust, will be effectual. . . . I can only say, in further apology, that if anything unhappy, which heaven forbid! shall have occurred to the person who, next to yourself, is dearest to me in this world, I shall have on my heart a subject of eternal regret."

**A Friendship loyal in spite of Disillusion.**—Mrs Gaskell,[1] with the grace and sincerity which distinguish her style, tells us of the friendship between Molly Gibson and Cynthia Fitzgerald. Molly is a charming English girl, sound of heart and sound of head, to whom comes the vision of Cynthia, beautiful and bewitching. Of course she fell in love with her half-sister (it is a mistake to suppose that girls fall in love with men only); while Cynthia was equally attracted by Molly's freshness and simplicity. Pleasant hours are passed in Mrs Gibson's drawing-room in chat and work. Both girls are kind, and each has a care for the interests of the other. There is the give-and-take of friendship between them; and, indeed, poor Molly is severely tried: Cynthia involves herself with men, and Molly endures many things to get her out of a dilemma. But she does endure them, without losing her own integrity; while Cynthia endures being obliged by her friend. But it is impossible to describe this natural friendship, not to be shattered by disillusion, in a few lines.

**Friends brought to us by the Circumstances of Life.**—It is a common error of youth to suppose that a friend must be a perfect person, and that the duty of loyalty ceases so soon as little failings show themselves. *David Copperfield*[2] offers a fine

---

[1] *Wives and Daughters,* by Mrs Gaskell.
[2] *David Copperfield*, by Charles Dickens.

study of the loyalties of life. David has a promiscuous collection of friends brought to him by the circumstances of his life; but how ready he is for the occasions of every one of them! With what simple good-humour he accepts Mr Micawber's description of him as 'the friend of my youth,' and Mrs Micawber's domestic confidences, when he himself was but a person of ten: how the Micawbers turn up at all sorts of inconvenient moments, and how they are always welcome to their friend: Traddles, too—what a nice person Traddles is; and what a sound and generous friendship exists between him and David! The list of friendships is a long one, the gradual ingathering of a life,—Peggotty, Mr Dick, Ham, Dr Strong, Mrs Peggotty, and the rest; in all he finds delight; all of them he honours, serves, and cherishes with entire loyalty. But not one of these friends dominates him or makes exclusive claims on his love. One friend he had with whom he lost his own individuality, who carried his heart by sheer fascination. Alas, this was Steerforth, and all the loyalty he could keep for him was that of a great sorrow over his friend's shame rather than over his death.

It is not the friends of our election who have exclusive claims upon us; the friends brought to us here and there by the circumstances of life all claim our loyalty, and from these we get, as did David Copperfield, kindness for kindness, service for service, loyalty for loyalty, full measure, heaped together and running over. One could hardly have a better guide in such matters than this charming tale of a life full of generous and loyal friendships, of fine chastity of soul, and containing, alas, the warning of a great unchastity!

# CHAPTER VI

## THE RULINGS OF CONSCIENCE IN THE HOUSE
## OF BODY: CHASTITY

### The Final Unchastity

IT all begins so innocently, and the end is so irremediably disastrous both to the man and the woman! People say it is one of the crying injustices of society that the woman should suffer and the man go 'scot-free.' But does he?

The confirmed profligate, perhaps, is not capable of further degradation; but the man who falls for the first time loses his future as certainly as the woman, if less obviously. He may escape public disgrace, but he never gets over the loss of power, purpose, and integrity which accompanies the loss of purity. He is handicapped for life, though he may himself have forgotten why; and should he at last marry, his children too often repeat their father's sin.

It is worth while to follow the history of a seduction as Mrs Gaskell gives it to us in *Ruth*. Ruth is a friendless orphan who is apprenticed to a milliner, and is distinguished among her fellow-apprentices by her quiet, lady-like manners and her beauty. "'I could not help knowing that I am pretty,' answered she simply, 'for many people have told me so.'"

She accompanies Mrs Mason, her employer, to
the shire ball, together with some other apprentices,
that they might be at hand to mend rents in the
ball dresses and the like; and a lady comes with
her fiance to have a tear mended. She is arrogant
to the young apprentice, and "Mr Bellingham looked
grave," and, at the end picking up a camellia, he
said: "Allow me, Miss Dunscombe, to give this in
your name to this young lady as thanks for her
dexterous help."

The reader admires Mr Bellingham for his act
of courtesy: and so, alas! does Ruth; the camellia
becomes a treasure, and the girl's thoughts dwell on
the courteous gentleman. Again she meets him, by
accident, in romantic circumstances. She is trying
to rescue a child from drowning, and he rides up and
succeeds in saving the boy. This leads to further
intercourse: he leaves his purse with Ruth to buy
what is necessary for the child, and of course she
has to see him again and account for what she has
spent. Then there are accidental meetings at church
—and still no wrong is intended. Next, the novelist
introduces us to Mr Bellingham at home:—

"His thoughts had been far more occupied by
Ruth than hers by him, although his appearance upon
the scene of her life was more an event to her than
to him . . . . He did not analyse the nature of his
feelings, but simply enjoyed them with the delight
which youth takes in experiencing new and strong
emotion. . . . The fact of his being an only child
had given him, as it does to many, a sort of in-
equality in those parts of the character which are
usually formed by the number of years a person
has lived. The unevenness of discipline to which

only children are subjected: the thwarting resulting from over-anxiety: the indiscreet indulgence arising from a love centred in one object—had been exaggerated in his education." In these few words the author gives us a key to the situation, and we begin to suspect what is to follow. Steerforth, too, in *David Copperfield*, was the only son of a proud, indulgent, and wayward mother; and Arthur Donnithorne, in *Adam Bede*—he, too, is the only son of a fond and imperious father. It would seem as if only children had more need than others to walk circumspectly; perhaps this is a fact, because in a commonwealth of brothers and sisters it is not quite easy to follow devious ways; and the devious ways are the danger, whether to one of a large family or to the only child. Young Bellingham finds himself fascinated, he does not know why, and all the more so because "there was a spell in the shyness which made her avoid and shun all admiring approaches to acquaintance. . . . By no over-bold admiration or rash, passionate word would he startle her. . . . In accordance with his determination, he resisted the strong temptation of walking by her side the whole distance home after church. He spoke a few words about the weather, bowed, and was gone. Ruth believed she should never see him again; and, in spite of sundry self-upbraidings for her folly, she could not help feeling as if a shadow had fallen on her life." Then comes a Sunday when Mr Bellingham walks home from church with her through the fields.

"'How strange it is,' she thought that evening, 'that I should feel as if this charming afternoon's walk were somehow, not exactly wrong, but yet as if it were not right!'" Other Sunday afternoon rambles follow.

The miseries she endures at Mrs Mason's are fully con-
fided; and then Bellingham wishes to see her old home,
Milham Grange, only six miles off. A fine Sunday
comes, and they go. He watched her with admiration
as she "wound in and out in natural, graceful, wavy
lines, between the luxuriant and overgrown shrubs."
All goes merrily until Mrs Mason, who is also out for
a Sunday holiday, finds Ruth in the young man's
company, and tells her she must never enter her doors
again. Her lover, who had left Ruth for a few
minutes, found her crying; and she told him what had
happened in the interval.

"Her eyes were so blinded by the fast-falling tears,
she did not see (nor, had she seen, would she have
been able to interpret) the change in Mr Bellingham's
countenance, as he stood silently watching her. He
was silent so long, that even in her sorrow she began
to wonder that he did not speak, and to wish to hear
his soothing words once more. 'It is very unfortunate,' he began, at last; and then he stopped; then he
began again, 'It is very unfortunate; for, you see, I
did not like to name it to you before, but I believe—I
have business, in fact, which obliges me to go to town
to-morrow—to London, I mean; and I don't know
when I shall be able to return.'" Hitherto, perhaps,
no more than dalliance had been intended; but such
dalliance is like the play of a little child on the brink
of a precipice. The novelist delicately marks the
moment, that moment of silence, when *lust* awoke as
a rage in the blood of the young man. Such a
moment of lust in the fairly right-meaning Arthur
Donnithorne led to the ruin of Hetty Sorrel and the
tragedy that followed it. The particular moment of
Steerforth's abandonment to his passions is not indi-

cated; but it is well that every young man and young woman should know that there is for *them*, as well as for everyone else, the possibility of being at death-grapple with that monster of our nature which we know as Lust. Self-indulgence prepares the way, dalliance offers a flowery by-path, and then, behold, before a person is aware, lust is upon him, and two lives are ruined. Safety lies, not in any immunity *we* may claim because we are refined, superior to common temptations; but in the strenuous, vigorous life of one who can say with St Paul, "I keep under my body and bring it into subjection." The primrose path of dalliance has only one end.

They go to London; but we next meet with them in North Wales. "'Indeed, and she's not his wife,' thought Jenny (the landlady of the inn); 'that's as clear as day.'" Still Ruth enjoyed the revelation, new to her, of mountain beauty, and "her admiration and her content made him angry"; she sighed a little "at her own want of power to amuse and occupy him she loved." The people at the inn comment upon the pair. "She's a very lovely creature," said one gentleman; "not above sixteen, I should think, very modest and innocent-looking in her white gown"; and his wife answered, "Well, I do think it's a shame such people should be allowed to come here." So thought others, and Ruth's lonely walks came to be annoyed by hostile notice. Next, Mr Bellingham falls ill of a fever, and his mother is sent for to nurse him; poor Ruth is thrown upon the scant kindness of the busy landlady, and endures days and nights of terrible anxiety; and when he mends, there is a long discussion with his mother as to Ruth. He

is weakly sorry, but chiefly sorry for himself; and
without seeing Ruth, without a word of farewell,
he says, "Could we not leave to-night? I should not
be so haunted by this annoyance in another place.
I dread seeing her again because I fear a scene;
and yet I believe I ought to see her in order to
explain." This was all he had to give for a ruined
life and for the unbounded devotion of a loving heart.
Ruth was so young and unsophisticated that we may
believe the full meaning of her offence had hardly
dawned upon her. The tale goes on, how mother
and son depart in great state, and he never seeks to
see her, or explain, or say a common farewell. A
good and grievously deformed man finds her afterwards, crouching in a lonely place; "and she said low
and mournfully, 'He has left me, sir!—sir, he has
indeed!—he has gone and left me!' Before he
could speak a word to comfort her, she had burst into
the wildest, dreariest crying ever mortal cried. The
settled form of the event, when put into words, went
sharp to her heart; her moans and sobs wrung his
soul; but, as no speech of his could be heard, if he
had been able to decide what best to say, he stood by
her in apparent calmness, while she, wretched, wailed
and uttered her woe. But when she lay worn out, and
stupefied into silence, she heard him say to himself in
a low voice, 'Oh, my God! for Christ's sake, pity
her!'" This good man and his sister nurse her
through a perilous illness, and at last take the poor
girl and her child with them to their home in Lancashire, where he is the minister of a small chapel.
Ruth went through the bitter waters of repentance,
and a life of penitence and humble service gave her
the beauty of Christian character; all the more

readily, no doubt, because her sin was rather the consequence of loneliness, despair and affection than of lust.

David, we know, discovered that there was forgiveness even for sins of lust; but they would seem to leave ineradicable marks in the character. So we find it in Mr Bellingham. Years after, when she was doing valued service in a subordinate position, Ruth met him again. "He was changed, she knew not how; in fact, the expression which had been only occasional formerly, when his worst self predominated, had become permanent. He looked restless and dissatisfied. . . . He thought that Mrs Denbigh" (the assumed name she went under) "was certainly like poor Ruth; but this woman was far handsomer . . . . Poor Ruth! and for the first time for several years he wondered what had become of her, though of course there was but one thing that could have happened; and perhaps it was as well he did not know her end, for most likely it would have made him very uncomfortable." This is Mr Bellingham as we get him after the lapse of years. Ruth, the sinned-against, was able to behave with Christian dignity and composure; while he, who was let off 'scot-free,' appears again in middle life—a man without aim, without conscience, and without heart, but a prey to consuming lust.

We need not follow the story to the end. It is well worth reading, the more so if the reader asks, with the Twelve, 'Lord, is it I?' Is this misery, or worse, this degradation of character, possible to me? Is there anything in me which could bring about so shameful a fall? Be assured there is.

Dark rumours reach our ears from time to time of white men in African wilds who have escaped from the restraints of civilisation and have broken out in acts of detestable cruelty. When we hear these things, too, let us say, 'Lord, is it I?' For it is true that, once we escape from the bonds of duty, our duty towards God and our duty towards our neighbour, lust and hate become rampant in us, and there is no fall of which we are not capable.

But let us take courage. No last fall can overtake him who keeps his soul from the first fall; who preserves his chastity as in that fabled tower of brass, and allows no image of uncleanness to sully his imagination; who keeps his mind, too, full of healthy interests and worthy employment; who keeps under his body, by self-compelled labours, and noble restraint as regards all laxity of eating and drinking, lounging and sleeping.

Such an one, knowing the perils that beset his way, prays steadfastly day by day, "Our Father which art in heaven, . . . lead us not into temptation, but deliver us from evil. Amen"; and, having prayed, he thinks no more of the matter, but goes on his way fearless and rejoicing in his life—

> "So keep I fair through faith and prayer
> A virgin heart in work and will."

# CHAPTER VII

## THE RULINGS OF CONSCIENCE IN THE HOUSE
## OF BODY: FORTITUDE

**Fortitude.**—Botticelli's picture of Fortitude, and
Ruskin's interpretation of it, are among the lessons
which Conscience should get by heart. This 'Fortitude' is no colossal figure, standing stark, bristling
with combative energy. Noble in stature, she yet
sits, weary after long-sustained effort; wistful, too, as
who should say, 'How long?' But, though resting,
she is wary and alert, still grasping the unsheathed
sword which lies across her knees. She is engaged
in a warfare whose end is not within sight; but hers
is not the joy of attack. She is weary indeed, yet
neither sorry for herself nor pleased with herself;
her regard is simple. She has the 'single eye' which
looks upon the thing to be done, not upon herself as
the doer—the thing to be borne, rather, for Fortitude
suffers.

The Bible hardly commends Fortitude to us by
name as a Christian grace, yet therein we shall
find our best exemplars. Our Lord, who bore more
than we are able to express, says of Himself, "I am
meek and lowly of heart"; and this saying, perhaps,
gives us a key to the meaning of Fortitude,—less

a valiant than a patient grace, memorable more for what she suffers gladly than for what she does.

As St Paul would image the fulness of Christ in the characters of Charity, so Isaiah gives us an image of Fortitude in setting forth the humiliation and sufferings of Christ. Fortitude grows up within us, a tender plant, is without form or comeliness, bears griefs and carries sorrows, endures chastisement, suffers and is dumb, does no violence, nor speaks deceit, is put to grief, yet—divides the spoil with the strong. There is only one true Fortitude among men, the fortitude of Christ; and every little bit of cheerful bearing that we are able for, without self-pity or self-complacency, comes of that divine fortitude.

Moses was the meekest man that ever lived, and his meekness was Fortitude. For forty years in the wilderness he bore with the waywardness of Israel; and, when the offences of the people had, so he thought, exceeded the patience of God, he prayed, "Yet now, if Thou wilt forgive their sin—; and if not, blot me also, I pray Thee, out of the Book of Life."

St Paul, too, after much bearing,—"in journeyings often; in perils of waters; in perils of robbers; in perils by mine own countrymen; in perils by the heathen; in perils in the city; in perils in the wilderness; in perils in the sea; in perils among false brethren; in weariness and painfulness; in watchings often; in hunger and thirst; in fastings often; in cold and nakedness,"—could wish that he, too, were accurst for his brethren.

Perhaps Fortitude has always an element of tenderness, and always means bearing for love's sake; if it be only the fortitude of a child who bears toothache cheerfully that he may not distress his mother.

The tradition of Fortitude was carried on in the Middle Ages rather in the school of chivalry—a school wherein the teachers were manifold distresses —than in the discipline and self-mortification of the monastery. Roland and Oliver, and each of the 'champions of Christendom,' has a record of distresses comparable with that of the Apostle. "Endure hardness," says St Paul to Timothy; and to endure without wincing and without resentment was a law of knightly bearing.

Sir Kenneth, in *The Talisman*,[1] brings home the notion of knightly Fortitude in a way possible for ourselves.

**Fortitude in Poverty.**—"'May I see your sick squire, fair sir?' The Scottish knight hesitated and coloured, yet answered at last, 'Willingly, my Lord of Gilsland; but you must remember, when you see my poor quarters, that the nobles and knights of Scotland feed not so high, sleep not so soft, and care not for the magnificence of lodgment, which is proper to their southern neighbours. I am *poorly* lodged, my Lord of Gilsland,' he added, with a haughty emphasis on the word, while, with some unwillingness, he led the way to his temporary place of abode. . . . Sir Kenneth cast a melancholy look around him, but suppressing his feelings, entered the hut, making a sign to the Baron of Gilsland to follow. . . . The interior of the hut was chiefly occupied by two beds. One was empty, but composed of collected leaves, and spread with an antelope's hide. It seemed, from the articles of armour laid beside it, and from a crucifix of silver, carefully and reverentially disposed at the head, to be the couch of the knight himself.

[1] By Sir Walter Scott.

The other contained the invalid, of whom Sir Kenneth had spoken, a strong-built and harsh-featured man, past, as his looks betokened, the middle age of life. His couch was trimmed more softly than his master's, and it was plain, that the more courtly garments of the latter, the loose robe, in which the knights showed themselves on pacific occasions, and the other little spare articles of dress and adornment, had been applied by Sir Kenneth to the accommodation of his sick domestic."

Here we have an example of Fortitude under very difficult circumstances, where pity and tenderness for dependants, personal dignity and high courage, go along with extreme poverty. The man who shows this manner of fortitude is a hero. The knight it is, and not that strange hermit-monk of the Lebanon, his body scarred with penitential wounds, who braces us by an example of Christian fortitude.

**Fortitude under Vexatious Provocations.—** Indeed, we are grateful for high lessons fitted to homely occasions, and we can at least understand how it was nothing less than high fortitude that Mrs Garth showed in the presence of an undeserved and vexatious calamity.

Mrs Garth[1] is at one and the same time making pies, superintending the baking and the washing, and teaching 'Lindley Murray' to her youngest boy and girl. Fred Vincy comes to see her husband, and, by and by, Caleb himself comes in.

"'Mrs Garth, I am come to tell something that I am afraid will give you a bad opinion of me. I am come to tell you and Mrs Garth that I can't keep my word. I can't find the money to meet the bill after

[1] *Middlemarch,* by George Eliot.

all. I have been unfortunate; I have only got these fifty pounds towards the hundred and sixty.'

"Mrs Garth was mutely astonished, and looked at her husband for an explanation. Caleb blushed, and after a little pause said—

"'Oh, I didn't tell you, Susan: I put my name to a bill for Fred; it was for a hundred and sixty pounds. He made sure he could meet it himself.'

"There was an evident change in Mrs Garth's face, but it was like a change below the surface of water which remains smooth. She fixed her eyes on Fred, saying—

"'I suppose you have asked your father for the rest of the money, and he has refused you.'

"'No,' said Fred, biting his lips, and speaking with more difficulty; 'but I know it will be of no use to ask him; and unless it were of use, I should not like to mention Mr Garth's name in the matter.'

"'It has come at an unfortunate time,' said Caleb, in his hesitating way, looking down at the notes and nervously fingering the paper. 'Christmas upon us— I'm rather hard up just now. You see, I have to cut out everything like a tailor with short measure. What can we do, Susan? I shall want every farthing we have in the bank. It's a hundred and ten pounds, the deuce take it!'

"'I must give you the ninety-two pounds that I have put by for Alfred's premium,' said Mrs Garth gravely and decisively, though a nice ear might have discerned a slight tremor in some of the words.

"'And I have no doubt that Mary has twenty pounds saved from her salary by this time. She will advance it.'

"Mrs Garth had not again looked at Fred, and was

not in the least calculating what words she should use to cut him the most effectively. Like the eccentric woman she was, she was at present absorbed in considering what was to be done, and did not fancy that the end would be better achieved by bitter remarks or explosions. But she had made Fred feel for the first time something like the tooth of remorse.

"'I shall certainly pay it all, Mrs Garth—ultimately,' he stammered out.

"'Yes, ultimately,' said Mrs Garth, who, having a special dislike to fine words on ugly occasions, could not now repress an epigram. 'But boys cannot well be apprenticed ultimately: they should be apprenticed at fifteen.' She had never been so little inclined to make excuses for Fred. . . . Fred turned and hurried out of the room.

"'I was a fool, Susan.'

"'That you were,' said the wife, nodding and smiling. 'But I should not have gone to publish it in the market-place. Why should you keep such things from me? It is just so with your buttons; you let them burst off without telling me, and go out with your wristband hanging.'"

Mrs Amos Barton[1] too—what a record of gentle and dignified fortitude is the story of her life and death in that poor parsonage house!

**Cheerful, Serviceable Fortitude.**—We think of Mark Tapley[2] with relief; he found 'no credit in being jolly' when things went well; but for cheerful, serviceable Fortitude, can any bit of knight-errantry exceed the 'jolly' way in which he made the best of things in 'Eden'? The foes he fought

[1] *Scenes of Clerical Life*, by George Eliot.
[2] *Martin Chuzzlewit*, by Charles Dickens.

were nothing more romantic than fever, famine, querulousness, heplessness in every member of that poor colony; and what a plucky, unostentatious fight it was! Mark Tapley deserves a place among our bosom friends; but he might think there was no credit in being jolly in so snug a niche.

Nor need we go to 'Eden' to find place for Fortitude. A birthday dinner cooked (!) by her loving family gave occasion to the 'old girl' (otherwise Mrs Bagnet, who is to be found in *Bleak House*[1]) for much cheerful serenity.

What a contrast she is, by the way, to Mrs Wilfer (*Our Mutual Friend*[1]), who lets the world know she is enduring by tying a black ribbon round her face. How many of us do the like with the metaphorical black ribbon of a sullen temper and a falling countenance! Instead of gradually ascending, we have come down from the high ideal of Fortitude to commonplace, even absurd, examples; but these fit our occasions; and it would not be a bad plan to keep a note-book recording the persons and incidents that give a fillip to conscience in this matter of Fortitude.

**The Roll of our Heroes.**—Time fails to tell of Nansen, Gordon, Howard, Livingstone, Collingwood, Raleigh, Galileo, Florence Nightingale, Calpurnia, Mackay of Uganda, Grace Darling; for the roll of persons notable for their Fortitude is, in fact, the roll of our heroes, and our little 'Book of Fortitude' will come to be a book of heroes, whether in small things or great. The reader will perhaps object that Fortitude belongs to the mind and the heart rather than to the body; but, when the body is not kept in

[1] By Charles Dickens.

its proper place, trained to endure without murmur, Fortitude has no chance. It is in the body we must endure hardness, and the training comes in the cheerful bearing of small matters not worth mentioning.

The *Song of the Lotos-Eaters* has music for us all:—

"All things have rest: why should we toil alone,
We only toil, who are the first of things,
And make perpetual moan,
Still from one sorrow to another thrown:
Nor ever fold our wings,
And cease from wanderings,
Nor steep our brows in slumber's holy balm;
Nor hearken what the inner spirit sings,
'There is no joy but calm!'
Why should we only toil, the roof and crown of things?"[1]

therefore we have need of Fortitude, without which no man or woman has ever yet brought life to any purpose: "So fight I, not as one that beateth the air: but I keep under my body, and bring it into subjection."

[1] Tennyson.

# CHAPTER VIII

## THE RULINGS OF CONSCIENCE IN THE HOUSE
## OF BODY: PRUDENCE

**Imprudence is Selfishness.**—"I, wisdom, dwell with prudence, and find out knowledge of witty inventions." Here is a saying worth pondering in an age when Prudence is not a popular grace. Young people confound rashness with generosity, and therefore hold Prudence in disfavour; when, of all cunning and injurious forms of selfishness, Imprudence is perhaps the most disastrous. Prudence is to be ranked among the K.C.s who instruct conscience concerning the affairs of the House of Body, because this virtue is exhibited for the most part in connection with material matters, and these all affect the body, directly or indirectly.

**Prudence in Affairs.**—We know the description of the virtuous woman; and, for virtuous, we might read prudent. It is Prudence who seeketh wool and flax and worketh diligently with her hands, who bringeth her food from afar. It is she who riseth early and giveth meat to her household, who considereth a field and buyeth it, who girdeth her loins with strength and strengtheneth her arms, who stretcheth out her hands to the poor, who is able to enrich her household, and to keep her place in the world with peace and honour.

Joseph was prudent. He looked ahead, and took measures for the advancement of his adopted country and the service of Pharaoh. Our own King Alfred was eminently prudent. Every great commander wins his battles as much through his prudence as his courage.

**Prudence in the Choice of a Friend.**—There was a time when Alcibiades[1] was prudent. "From the first he was surrounded with pleasures, and a multitude of admirers determined to say nothing but what they thought would please, and to keep him from all admonition and reproof; yet, by his native penetration, he distinguished the value of Socrates, and attached himself to him, rejecting the rich and great who sued for his regard. With Socrates he soon entered into the closest intimacy; and finding that he did not, like the rest of the unmanly crew, want improper favours, but that he studied to correct the errors of his heart, and to cure him of his empty and foolish arrogance,—

> Then his crest fell, and all his pride was gone,
> He droop'd the conquered wing.

In fact, he considered the discipline of Socrates as a provision from heaven for the preservation and benefit of youth. Thus, despising himself, admiring his friend, adoring his wisdom, and revering his virtue, he insensibly formed in his heart the image of love, or rather came under the influence of that power, who, as Plato says, secures his votaries from vicious love."

[1] Plutarch's Life of Alcibiades.

Here we have a fine example of prudence in the choice of a friend and mentor, and well had it been for Alcibiades had his constancy been equal to his prudence.

**Prudence rejects Undue Influence.**—Alexander,[1] in his heroic days, showed admirable prudence. He was able to distinguish between things that differ, that is, he understood the relative importance of the matters that came before him. "As for his mother, he made her many magnificent presents, but he would not suffer her busy genius to exert itself in state affairs, or in the least to control the proceedings of government. She complained of this as a hardship, and he bore her ill-humour with great mildness. Antipater once wrote him a long letter full of heavy complaints against her, and when he had read it he said, 'Antipater knows not that one tear of a mother can blot out a thousand such complaints.'" Not even his mother might interfere with the duties of his office, and yet how tender was his love for her!

We know how a greater than Alexander said, "Wist ye not that I must be about my Father's business?" and it is eminently the part of Prudence to allow of no undue influence in any public capacity even from our nearest and dearest; because we are called upon to think, *ourselves*, for the good of all concerned, and not to be influenced by the private interests of any. There is something rotten in any state whose officers can be induced to act for the private good of themselves or their belongings.

Prudence chooses simplicity and eschews luxury, finds more honour in labours than in pleasures, trains the body to endure hardness. In all these respects

[1] Plutarch's *Life of Alexander.*

we find in Alexander an example of gentle, heroic
prudence.

**Prudence Temperate in all Things.**—"He found
that his great officers set no bounds to their luxury,
that they were most extravagantly delicate in their
diet, and profuse in other respects; insomuch that
Agnon of Teos *wore silver* nails in his shoes;
Leonatus had many camel-loads of earth brought
from Egypt to rub himself with when he went to the
wrestling-ring; Philotas had hunting-nets that would
enclose the space of a hundred furlongs; more made
use of rich essences than oil after bathing, and had
their grooms of the bath, as well as chamberlains who
excelled in bed-making. This degeneracy he reproved
with all the temper of a philosopher. He told them,
'It was very strange to him that, after having undergone
so many glorious conflicts, they did not remember
that those who come from labour and exercise always
sleep more sweetly than the inactive and effeminate;
and that, in comparing the Persian manners with the
Macedonian, they did not perceive that *nothing was
more servile than the love of pleasure, or more princely
than a life of toil.* How will that man,' continued he,
'take care of his own horse, or furbish his lance and
helmet, whose hands are too delicate to wait on his
own dear person? Know you not that the end of
conquest is, not to do what the conquered have done,
but something greatly superior?'" [1]

**Prudent Citizens the Wealth of the State.**—
The laws of Lycurgus[2] were the outcome of a noble
and generous prudence. If Sparta were to hold its own
in the long conflict with Athens, it must be through

[1] Plutarch's *Life of Alexander.*
[2] Plutarch's *Life of Lycurgus.*

the fitness of its individual citizens. Lycurgus recognised that each citizen possessed in himself the wealth most valuable to the state, in a body fit for toil and endurance, and a mind capable of seeing 'the proportion of things.

"Desirous to complete the conquest of luxury and exterminate the love of riches, he introduced a third institution which was wisely enough and ingeniously contrived. This was the use of public tables where all were to eat in common of the same meat, and such kinds of it as were appointed by law. At the same time, they were forbidden to eat at home upon expensive couches and tables, to call in the assistance of butchers and cooks, or to fatten like voracious animals in private. For so not only their manners would be corrupted, but their bodies disordered; abandoned to all manner of sensuality and dissoluteness, they would require long sleep, warm baths, and the same indulgence as in perpetual sickness . . . . Another ordinance, levelled against magnificence and expense, directed that the ceilings of the houses should be wrought with no tool but the axe, and the doors with nothing but the saw. For as Epaminondas is reported to have said afterwards, of his table, *Treason lurks not under such a dinner*, so Lycurgus perceived, before him, that such a house admits of no luxury and needless splendour. Indeed, no man could be so absurd as to bring into a dwelling so homely and simple, bedsteads with silver feet, purple coverlets, golden cups, and a train of expense that follows these; but all would necessarily have the bed suitable to the room, the coverlet of the bed and the rest of their utensils and furniture to that."

There are many points in which a Christian

commonwealth may not emulate the Spartan regi-
men; but wise men are feeling strongly that
prudence requires of us, for the good of the state,
to live simple lives, to avoid excesses, even if they
come in the way of athletic or intellectual toils,
and to eschew possessions more than are necessary
for fit and simple living. Perhaps it is lawful for
us to allow ourselves, in our furniture and implements,
beauty of form and colour, and fitness for our uses;
but it may be our duty not to accumulate unnecessary
possessions, the care of which becomes a responsibility,
and whose value lies in their costliness. These things
interfere with that real wealth of a serviceable body
and alert mind which we owe to the service of our
country as well as that of our home.

"When the money was brought to Athens, Phocion[1]
asked the persons employed in that commission
'Why, among all the citizens of Athens, he should
be singled out as the object of such bounty?'
'Because,' said they, 'Alexander looks upon you as
the only honest and good man.' 'Then,' said Phocion,
'let him permit me always to retain that character,
as well as really to be that man.' The envoys then
went home with him, and, when they saw the frugality
that reigned there, his wife baking bread, himself
drawing water and afterwards washing his own feet,
they urged him the more to receive the present.
They told him, 'It gave them real uneasiness, and
was indeed an intolerable thing, that the friend of
so great a prince should live in such a wretched
manner.' At that instant a poor old man happening
to pass by, in a mean garment, Phocion asked the
envoys, 'Whether they thought worse of him than

[1] Plutarch's *Life of Phocion.*

of that man?' As they begged of him not to make such a comparison, he rejoined, 'Yet that man lives upon less than I do, and is contented. In one word, it will be to no purpose for me to have so much money if I do not use it; and if I was to live up to it, I should bring both myself and the king, your master, under the censure of the Athenians.' Thus the money was carried back from Athens, and the whole transaction was a good lesson to the Greeks, that the man who did not want such a sum of money was richer than he who could bestow it."

In the matter of Prudence, also, our Master shows us the better way. It was written of Christ, "My servant shall deal prudently"; and we should find great profit in studying the Gospel histories to see how our Lord dealt prudently with that possession of His personal life, the sole possession He allowed to Himself, and the sole possession of value to which any of us can attain. Thinking upon Christ, we shall walk soberly, and not run into any excess of riot.

# CONSCIENCE IN THE HOUSE OF MIND

## CHAPTER IX

### OPINIONS 'IN THE AIR'

EVERYBODY knows that the affairs of his body and those of his heart should be ordered by his conscience. Our acts and feelings towards other people, and our management of our own bodies, fall, we believe, properly under the judgment of Conscience; but we have a notion that thought is free; that, in the domain of intellect, every man is his own master, and that the opinions we form, the mental work we choose to do or to leave undone, are beyond the pale of duty. *Thought is free*, is our unconscious watchword.

**Casual Opinions.**—Now, of all the errors that have hindered men and nations, this is perhaps the most unfortunate. A man picks up a notion, calls it his opinion, spreads it here and there, until in the end that foolish notion becomes a danger to society and a bondage to the individual. "These be thy gods, O Israel!" is a cry that is constantly rising in our camp. We do not know in whose tent it began, but opinion flashed a lightning message over all the camp of Israel, and every man brought his precious things for the making of the golden calf. Why? Their leader was out of sight for the moment—with God, it is true, but, still, out of sight, and the tribes made haste to worship at a shrine of their own invention. This story typifies the sudden inroad of opinion by which nations and persons are apt to be carried away. The lawgiver fails to direct, and clamorous opinion fills the ear.

In the summer holidays, when people have not much to think about, the newspapers lend themselves to the discussion of such idle questions as, 'Is life worth living?' 'Is marriage a failure?'—the under lying opinion being that life is not worth living, and marriage is a failure. Sensible people laugh at these letters; but there are many who lie in wait for any chance notion that comes floating their way, take it up zealously, and make it their business in life to spread it.

When such minds get hold of the idea that marriage is a failure, for example, much immorality is the result. The notion has become the molten calf; the lawgiver, Conscience, is away or silenced; and people think it rather a fine thing to make sacrifices for the idea they cherish at the moment. Or, again, they go about asking, 'Is life worth living?' and though the results may seem less grave because less criminal, they are really as serious. That people should be sullen and ungrateful for rain and sunshine, food and raiment, the beauty of the world and the kindness of friends, is not a crime, because it is not one of the offences against society punishable by law; but it is a black sin, as catching as the plague, and he has caught it who allows himself to ask, 'Is life worth living?'

**How Fallacies work.**—We know, by hearsay, how the 'killing-no-murder' fallacy works; how apparently good men, who let in the notion, are convinced by their own Reason that the death of an offender against the liberties of the people is the only safety for the rest; that providence has called them to the great task, that they will be regarded thenceforth as the deliverers of their people. They kill the man, and are abhorred by all thinking persons as assassins. How has it come about?

Conscience, which thunders, 'THOU SHALT DO NO MURDER,' had been silenced; Opinion played the part of director, Reason supported Opinion, and the shameful deed was done. The slightest waft of opinion is enough to mislead the open, or rather the *empty*, mind. The newspaper headings displayed day by day are enough. 'The Unreality of Sin' figured in a local newspaper the other day (anent certain American teaching). Anyone who is aware of the hunger of the unoccupied mind for any chance deposit of ideas will realise how such a heading would be accepted by many minds, and cherished as a sanction for sin.

When I was a girl the darning of stockings was considered a great piece of domestic virtue; and, one day, I heard a Welsh lady of staidness and moral correctness say that she did not believe in darning stockings! I found out afterwards that the darning she meant was running the heels of new stockings; but I seized on the doctrine as applying to all manner of holes, with a great sense of emancipation. It is just so that chance sayings about more important matters are caught up and acted upon. There is ever some new fallacy in the air which allures its thousands, and no one is safe who is not cognisant of danger, and who does not know how to safeguard himself. Perhaps no rules for the right conduct of life are more important than the following: (*a*) that we may not play with chance opinions; (*b*) that our own Reason affords an insufficient test of the value of an opinion (because Reason, as we have seen, argues in behalf of Inclination); (*c*) that we must labour to get knowledge as the foundation of opinions; (*d*) that we must also labour to arrive at principles whereby to try our opinions.

# CHAPTER X

## THE UNINSTRUCTED CONSCIENCE

THERE is no end to the vagaries of the uninstructed conscience. It is continually straining out the gnat and swallowing the camel. The most hardened criminal has his conscience; and he justifies that which he does by specious reasons. 'Society is against' him, he says; he 'has never had a fair chance.' Why should he 'go about ragged and hungry when another man rides in his carriage and eats and drinks his fill?' 'If that man has so much, let him keep it if he can; if cleverer wits than his contrive to ease him of a little, that is only fair play!' Thus do reason and inclination support one another in the mind of the Ishmael whose hand is against every man; and, if every man's hand is against him, that is all the more reason, he urges, that he should get what he can take out of life.

**Conscience Persistent upon some Points.**—But there are points upon which the glib flow of reason does not silence his conscience. He must be true to his 'pals,' and to give up a pal to justice would probably be a greater crime in his eyes than to kill a man. Also, he will be fair in his dealings with his companions, and will share according to bargain. Perhaps he has a child whom he cherishes, or a friend whom he cares for. No man's conscience is silent on every point of duty; and perhaps there is no one, savage or civilised, who does not act up to his conscience in, at any rate, some few points. The first effort of the missionary or explorer is to find out in what matters the people he is amongst are dependable. Livingstone was able to live with the most degraded tribes of Africans, because his sympathy and knowledge helped him to discover safe ground,—the points on which the savage conscience was inflexible, as, for example, loyalty to a guest, gratitude to a benefactor. Indeed, Livingstone made some great discoveries in human nature amongst these barbarous tribes; for the good that is true of the worst must be true of those who are better. He found they all knew that they must not murder, nor steal, must be obedient to parents, kind to each other, and much besides; that is to say, they had the light of conscience. We know, too, from Captain Cook how the Otaheitans wept when they first saw a white man flogged. Cruelty was contrary to their savage code.

**Moral Stability.**—But the uninstructed conscience is open to every prompting of inclination, seconded, as it is sure to be, by a thousand good reasons. This is the cause of the instability of conduct shown by the savage, the criminal, the raw schoolboy, the rough yokel, and the ignorant and undisciplined of every class of life, even when such ignorance is credited by a university degree. It is only the instructed conscience which is stable.

There are persons of whom we say, 'We always know how so-and-so will act. We can *depend* upon him.' The reason is that he is not liable to be carried away by sudden inroads of outside opinion.

His knowledge affords him a standard by which he judges the worth of such opinion; his principles, a test of its moral rightness. Therefore the flashy new opinion, which history tells him has been tried and found wanting long ago, has no chance with him. He examines it in the light of his principles, finds it to be based on an error of thought, that it leads to further errors of thought and action; and it takes no hold upon his mind.

**A Nation may be Unstable.**—As for the rest—the persons who have taken no pains to instruct their conscience—the sudden rush of a community, a person, a nation after a new notion, the last crank, is extraordinary, and becomes a mania. Scott, who is a past master in moral philosophy, perhaps because of his legal habit of mind, gives us in *Peveril of the Peak* an historical example of the nation run mad with a notion. And a single example of the power of a notion on the uninstructed conscience, and of how such baseless notion may spread like an epidemic, is so instructive that I must quote part of a note relative to the Popish Plot appended to *Peveril of the Peak*:—"The infamous character of those who contrived and carried on the pretended Popish Plot, may be best estimated by the account given in North's *Examen*, who describes Oates himself with considerable power of colouring. 'He was now in his trine exaltation, his Plot in full force, efficacy and virtue; he walked about with his guards (assigned for fear of the Papists murdering him). He had lodgings in Whitehall, and £1200 per annum pension: and no wonder, after he had the impudence to say to the House of Lords, in plain terms, that, if they would not help him to more money, he must be forced to help himself. He put on an Episcopal garb (except the lawn sleeves), silk gown and cassock, great hat, satin hatband and rose, long scarf, and was called, or most blasphemously called himself, the Saviour of the nation; whoever he pointed at, was taken up and committed; so that many people got out of his way, as from a blast. . . . The very breath of him was pestilential, and, if it brought not imprisonment or death over such on whom it fell, it surely poisoned reputation . . . . The Queen herself was accused at the Commons' bar. The city, for fear of the Papists, put up their posts and chains; and the Chamberlain, Sir Thomas Player, in the Court of Aldermen, gave his reason for the city's using that caution, which was, that he did not know but the next morning they might all rise with their throats cut. . . . Nothing ordinary or moderate was to be heard in people's communication; but every debate and action was high-flown and tumultuous. All freedom of speech was taken away; and not to believe the Plot, was worse than being Turk, Jew, or infidel.'"

**A Besetting Idea.**—This theme seems to have had some fascination for the mind of Scott. He presents it to us as the key to more than one historical character. In Balfour of Burley,[1] we have a monomaniac, a man possessed and impelled by a homicidal idea; and yet, when that idea had resulted in barbarous and sacrilegious crime, the man's native, uninstructed conscience wrestled with the 'reasonable' conclusion to which he had brought himself, and he suffered great mental anguish. This example of a besetting idea is even more instructive than that of Brutus, as Shakespeare interprets him, because Scott

[1] *Old Mortality.*

is at some pains to show that prejudice, credulousness, intolerance, superstition, lawless ambition, even homicidal crime, are the natural outcome of the dark mind of ignorance; the more so, when this ignorance is allied with mental power, and the mind is struck by a forcible idea. The belated action of conscience upon such a mind is portrayed in this case with wonderful vividness.

The same author brings again before us the perils of benighted ignorance, and its power of converting the purest teaching to the foulest uses, in the character of the Independent, Sergeant Tomkins[1] (or, as he calls himself, Honest Joe and Trusty Tomkins), who believed that he was saved, and therefore could do no sin; which he interpreted to mean that that which was foul sin in other men, he might commit and yet be void of offence.

**Perils of Ignorance.**—In our own days of enlightenment and progress, we seem to be less aware of the grossness, dulness and foulness of ignorance than were the more thoughtful minds of the Middle Ages. We do not understand that the uninstructed conscience is at the mercy of the darkened mind. Intelligent persons will be heard to remark, 'I don't see the good of missionaries,' 'Every nation and tribe has the religion best suited to it'; as though anything but evil can come out of the dark places of the earth, where passion, prejudice, and superstition extinguish the natural light of Conscience.

The ignorance at home, in our very schools and colleges, is a cause of alarm. It is because of our ignorance that we are like those seventy thousand Americans whom Emerson describes as "going about in search of a religion."' The very 'tolerance' upon

[1] *Woodstock.*

which we pride ourselves arises from the ignorance which does not know how to distinguish between things that differ. We are not so far gone, perhaps, as that nation which provides us with new notions and new religions, but our readiness to receive what comes in our way lays us open to the charge of an uninstructed conscience.

In political matters we trust to our newspaper, which is expressly the organ of our party, and do not look for the side-lights of other writings, or the illumination cast by history and literature. We get our education in this kind out of compendiums and lectures; and these, naturally, cannot afford the copious detail out of which conscience gathers instruction.

**Scrupulosity.**—We are in the way, too—like that young man of whom Mrs Piozzi tells us in her *Anecdotes* of Johnson,—of erring by over-scrupulosity in one direction, as by laxity in another.

"A person," Johnson said, "had for these last five weeks often called at my door, but would not leave his name or any other message, but that he wished to speak with me. At last we met, and he told me that he was oppressed by scruples of conscience. I blamed him gently for not applying, as the rules of our Church direct, to his parish priest or other discreet clergyman; when, after some compliments on his part, he told me he was clerk to a very eminent trader, at whose warehouses much business consisted in packing goods in order to go abroad; that he was often tempted to take paper and packthread for his own use, and that he had indeed done so often, that he could recollect no time when he had ever bought any for himself. 'But probably,' said I, 'your master was wholly indifferent with regard to such trivial emoluments. You had better ask for it at once, and so take your trifles with content.' 'Oh, sir!' replies the visitor, 'my master bid me have as much as I pleased, and was half angry when I talked to him about it.' 'Then pray, sir,' said I, 'tease me no more about such airy nothings,' and was going on to be very angry, when I recollected that the fellow might be mad, perhaps; so I asked him, 'When he left the counting-house of an evening?' 'At seven o'clock, sir.' 'And when do you go to bed, sir?' 'At twelve o'clock.' 'Then,' replied I, 'I have at least learnt thus much by my new acquaintance—that five hours of the four-and-twenty unemployed are enough for a man to go mad in; so I would advise you, sir, to study algebra, if you are not already an adept in it. Your head would get less muddy, and you will leave off tormenting your neighbours about paper and packthread, while we all live together in a world that is bursting with sin and sorrow.'"

Undue scrupulosity about small matters is a sure mark of the uninstructed conscience. The man should not have taken his master's packthread; but to occupy his own attention and that of others about so small a matter was a worse offence, and illustrates the fact that only the instructed conscience is capable of seeing things in due proportion, of distinguishing what really matters from that which is of no consequence. This is why a child makes such enormous mistakes in his valuation of life. He will be guilty of lying, unkindness, cruelty even, and not know that he has done wrong, while a trifling act, like the opening of a forbidden drawer, will fret his conscience for months. The schoolboy's moral code is marked by similar disproportion. To deceive his master is no offence, but to 'blab' on another boy puts him beyond the pale.

The subject of the uninstructed conscience is so wide, and covers so much of life, that I can only offer an illustration or a hint here and there; but let us be sure of this, that, though all men are endowed with conscience, its light is steady and certain only in proportion as it is informed by a cultivated intelligence; and of this, also, that the uninstructed conscience leaves its possessor open to bigotry, fanaticism, panic, envy, spite. His reason justifies every offence to a man who has little knowledge of persons and events whereby to correct his judgments. You will observe, I am not speaking of *wilful sin*; alas, the instructed conscience also is open to sin! But we shall consider this most anxious matter later: meantime, let us be well assured that more than half the errors and offences committed in the world are sins of ignorance; that is, people think and do amiss because they are at no pains to acquire an instructed conscience.

# CHAPTER XI

## THE INSTRUCTED CONSCIENCE

**Sound Moral Judgment.**—I do not say that the man with the instructed conscience is incapable of moral wrong. That is not the case. His advantage is that he can rarely do or think amiss without being aware of his offence; and the stability which this enlightenment gives to its possessor is a distinction. Emerson remarks upon the curious fact that many persons have a name, a force, in the world which exceeds their deeds or their recorded words. We are profoundly interested in Arnold Toynbee, John Sterling, Arthur Hallam, and other young men whose span of life did not by much exceed their university days. Emerson says that the secret of this sort of esteem which is not founded upon accomplishment is—character. Very likely he is right; but perhaps the particular development of character we reverence in such men is the sound moral judgment born of the instructed conscience. Goldsmith gives us a charming type of this manner of moral balance in Dr Primrose.[1] How wise are his decisions, how just his resolutions, how gentle and how penetrating his reproofs. Can we ever forget that epitaph to which his wife should live up, or the

[1] *The Vicar of Wakefield*

way in which he allowed his family to have that portrait painted—too big for any room in the house—a reproof of vanity none of them could forget! How humble he is in prosperity, how equable in adversity! And all this has come to him through his books and his prayers—not through his books alone, and not through his prayers alone.

Dr Johnson,[1] too. We who are used to dictionaries are not impressed by 'the great lexicographer' as such. Indeed, his output, whether in action or in writing, was surprisingly small for a man of such vast power; and, as to the manner of his writing, why, Boswell himself had a style that we like better to-day; but there have been few men better qualified than he to arrive at the just judgments of an instructed conscience. That is why the *Life* is such inimitable reading. To be plied with Boswell's 'Sir?' on all manner of occasions must have been irritating, and we do not wonder that now and then Johnson whimsically chose to make the worse appear the better cause. But what a world of just and righteous judgments the wise man utters! No wonder his contemporaries waited on his words. We can all talk platitudes and air the moralities of others; but to say what he himself would call 'luminous' things about all the occasions of life, many of the personages in history—this is a distinction to which only the instructed conscience can enable a man to attain. It is probable that everyone who makes his mark beyond what we see of his accomplishment does so from the force, not of genius, but of moral judgment.

**Moral Judgments and a Virtuous Life.**—The power to form moral judgments and the power to live

[1] Boswell's *Life of Johnson*

a virtuous life are not identical; but for persons whose living is not confined to a very narrow sphere the one is necessary to the other. Simple people may think duly about daily work and duties because their conscience is instructed by homely wisdom that has come down to them without their knowing it; but, if we mean to live in the wide world of thought and action, our first care must be to get, by slow degrees, the power of forming just opinions.

How are we to get such power? In the first place, we must observe and think for ourselves, not 'cute' and clever thoughts about our neighbours' doings, discovering a low motive here, a sharp practice there: persons who allow themselves in this habit of mind lose the power of interpreting life by the aid of an illuminated conscience. But, if we observe with gentle, large, and humble thoughts, we shall find much to instruct and improve us in the life of every family. We shall see good in the action of statesmen, at home and abroad; wisdom in the attitudes of nations.

But most of us have little chance of seeing men and things on a wide scale, and our way to an instructed conscience is to read, mark, learn, and inwardly digest. We must read novels, history, poetry, and whatever falls under the head of literature, not for our own 'culture.' Some of us begin to dislike the word 'culture,' and the idea of a 'cultivated' person; any effort which has self as an end is poor and narrow. But there is a better reason for an intimacy with literature as extensive and profound as we can secure. Herein we shall find the reflections of wise men upon the art of living, whether put in the way of record, fable, or precept, and this is the chief art for us all to attain.

# CHAPTER XII

## SOME INSTRUCTORS OF CONSCIENCE: POETRY, NOVELS, ESSAYS

**Poetry.**—Poetry is, perhaps, the most searching and intimate of our teachers. To know *about* such a poet and his works may be interesting, as it is to know about repousse work; but in the latter case we must know how to use the tools before we get joy and service out of the art. Poetry, too, supplies us with tools for the modelling of our lives, and the use of these we must get at for ourselves. The line that strikes us as we read, that recurs, that we murmur over at odd moments—this is the line that influences our living, if it speak only—

> "Of old, unhappy, far-off things,
> And battles long ago."

A couplet such as this, though it appear to carry no moral weight, instructs our conscience more effectually than many wise saws. As we 'inwardly digest,' reverence comes to us unawares, gentleness, a wistful tenderness towards the past, a sense of continuance, and of a part to play that shall not be loud and discordant, but of a piece with the whole. This is one of the 'lessons never learned in schools' which comes to each of us only as we discover it for ourselves.

Many have a favourite poet for a year or two, to be discarded for another and another. Some are happy enough to find the poet of their lifetime in Spenser, Wordsworth, Browning, for example; but, whether it be for a year or a life, let us mark as we read, let us learn and inwardly digest. Note how good this last word is. What we digest we assimilate, take into ourselves, so that it is part and parcel of us, and no longer separable.

We probably read Shakespeare in the first place for his stories, afterwards for his characters, the multitude of delightful persons with whom he makes us so intimate that afterwards, in fiction or in fact, we say, 'She is another Jessica,' and 'That dear girl is a Miranda'; 'She is a Cordelia to her father,' and, such a figure in history, 'a base Iago.' To become intimate with Shakespeare in this way is a great enrichment of mind and instruction of conscience. Then, by degrees, as we go on reading this world-teacher, lines of insight and beauty take possession of us, and unconsciously mould our judgments of men and things and of the great issues of life.

**Novels.**—Novels, again, are as homilies to the wise; but not if we read them merely for the tale. It is a base waste of time to read a novel that you can skip, or that you look at the last page of to see how it ends. One must read to learn the meaning of life; and we should know in the end, who said what, and on what occasion! The characters in the books we know become our mentors or our warnings, our instructors always; but not if we let our mind behave as a sieve, through which the whole slips like water.

It would, of course, be a foolish waste of time to give this sort of careful reading to a novel that has neither literary nor moral worth, and therefore it is well to confine ourselves to the best—to novels that we can read over many times, each time with increased pleasure. The superficial way in which people read is illustrated by the fact that ninety-nine out of a hundred run away with the notion that Thackeray presents us with Amelia[1] as an ideal woman; while few extract the solemn moral of the tale—that a man cannot give to a woman more than she is worth; and that Dobbin, the faithful Dobbin, found his life at last, not in Amelia, but in his books and his daughter. It is well that we should choose our authors with judgment, as we choose our friends, and then wait upon them respectfully to hear what they have to say to us.

**Essays.**—Of the ever-delightful essayists, I will not speak here. These, like the poets, we must find out for ourselves. They make a claim of special personal intimacy with their readers, and each apparently light phrase should give us pause: there may be more in it than meets the eye. Anyway, the essayist, to take him at his best, writes because he has something personal to say to you and me, because there is some fruit of the thought of his life he would have us taste; so let us read for edification.

[1] *Vanity Fair.*

# CHAPTER XIII

## SOME INSTRUCTORS OF CONSCIENCE: HISTORY AND PHILOSOPHY

**History.**—History, including the lives of historical personages, approaches us on other ground. The passion of patriotism, the bond of citizenship, are dominant in our age, perhaps because the new imperial idea has taken hold of us; but still more, perhaps, because we are in the rebound from the individualism of the preceding generation. Let us be thankful that we are moved by these strong forces; but their very strength may hurry us into presumptuous sins, unless we recognise our position with regard to country and city, and labour for the instructed conscience.

**The Informed Patriot.**—We must read our newspaper, of course—newspapers on both sides; but he who founds upon his newspaper is an ignorant patriot and an illiberal citizen. His opinions are no more than parrot-like repetitions of other men's sayings; whereas he who dwells with dutiful interest upon the history of his own country, distressed over her ignominies, proud when she has shown herself great; who has pondered the history of another great empire—admiring the temperate justice with which its distant colonies were administered, and scrutinising the causes of its fall—he gradually acquires some insight as to the meaning of national life. He is able to express an opinion which is not a mere echo, and gains convictions which will certainly be of use to his country, even if they are known only to the people about his own fireside.

He learns to esteem Xerxes as a great gardener, a planter, whose aim it was that every man should have his little 'paradise.' Lycurgus is to him more than a lawgiver, he is a hero able to keep the laws he made. Such a person regards, with half-envious interest, the records of those small yet great republics, distinguished in the arts of peace and of war, in whose open schools every man picked up philosophy, and the best men made it the study of a lifetime.

He who reads history in this way, not to pass examinations, nor to obtain culture, nor even for his own pleasure (delightful as such reading is), but because he knows it to be his duty to his country to have some intelligent knowledge of the past, of other lands as well as of his own, must add solid worth to the nation that owns him. It is something to prepare for the uses of the State a just, liberal, and enlightened patriotism in the breast of a single citizen.

**Philosophy.**—Philosophy lays her hand upon us, as upon the youth of Athens, with an absolute claim. We are remarkable among the civilised peoples for our ignorance of what has been already thought in the world, has been given up as futile, or has passed into common knowledge. For five thousand years, at least, philosophers have been in search of a single principle which shall cover, to put it crudely, matter and mind. We think, to-day, that we have found this principle in evolution. It may be so; but we allow ourselves to come to the conclusion without due knowledge of what has been already thought, without even taking in the fact that, if we accept the doctrine *as including the evolution of mind*, we give up the idea that there is any life here or hereafter excepting physical life, any existence beyond a physical existence. I do not propose to discuss this thesis; all I say is, that we should not lay ourselves open blindfold to such far-reaching conclusions, in the belief that things must be thus and thus because another man's reason has found them so; our own reason, taking his lead, finding them so too. Let us perceive and know with certainty that the function of reason is to bring us to the logical conclusion of any premises we think it well to receive.

Then we shall see that it rests with us to choose the notions which we are willing to admit to reasonable proof; and to make this choice, conscience must be instructed. The history of thought will bring us abundant evidence of the fallibility of reason; therefore, there is no certainty that what proves itself to us must be right. Approximate certainty lies in two directions—in a knowledge of the history of the thought of the past, and in a carefully calculated forecast of the issues. We must reach our convictions, not through our own reasoning, or another man's, however conclusive; but reason must work upon knowledge, and be instructed by a wide survey of all that is involved. The person who refuses to be influenced by what has gone before and what will follow, embraces what he calls 'the truth' in a spirit of ignorant partisanship.

Columbus, we know, received an idea that was, no doubt, floating in the air, the idea of a western passage to the Indies. After attempts in other quarters, he brought his idea to Ferdinand and Isabella; they gave it generous reception, and provided him with ships and money. But he would have been a mere adventurer had he come with no more than a notion that proved itself to his own understanding. He was armed with the history of the voyages of the past, which showed that his particular adventure had not been accomplished; with a knowledge of geographical principles, which proved his notion tenable; with a forecast of the results of his discovery, should he succeed; that is, he was able conscientiously to lay his scheme before the Spanish monarchs, and the result justified him.

We cannot escape from the necessity for knowledge, especially in this realm of ideas. The thousand quack philosophies of the day—as of all past days—have their birth in minds ignorant of the thought of the past, and unaware of the fact when they are offering a patched-up version of ideas and principles which have already been found wanting.

**A 'Message.'**—Many men believe that they have a message, become fanatics for their message, and make—nothing is so easy—innumerable converts. But not every notion is a message. Such indications come, as Coleridge has finely said, to minds "already prepared to receive them by a higher Power than Nature herself." As for the preparation,—knowledge, insight, foresight, and the meekness of wisdom, the gentleness of one under guidance,—these are signs by which we can discern, each for himself, if we, indeed, have a message, or (for this also is a mission) are prepared to take up and carry forward a message. The messages are manifold, the messengers are many; but few things hinder the progress of the world more than the wilful and fanatical adoption of notions because they appeal to us, and because our own reason proves them right. The secret of safety in matters of philosophy, as well as in all practical matters of life, is to know that we *are capable of being convinced of anything*, however wrong or foolish, unless we are able to bring an instructed conscience to the consideration of the acceptable notion.

# CHAPTER XIV

## SOME INSTRUCTORS OF CONSCIENCE: THEOLOGY

**Theology.**—Theology, divinity, the knowledge of God, by whatever name we call it, is a sphere in which, more than any other, we must needs be ruled by the instructed conscience; and yet we are apt to think, as do the children, that God requires us to be good, and punishes us when we are bad; and this is all we care to know about religion: we leave out of count that knowledge of God which, we have it on the authority of Christ himself, 'is eternal life.'

Perhaps it is because the word 'eternal' casts our thoughts into the far future, about which we do not much concern ourselves. We do not realise that eternity is past, present, and to come. Life, in any real sense, is the knowledge of God now; and, without that knowledge, there cannot be the free and joyous activity of our powers, the glow of our feelings, the happy living, free from care, the open eye for all beauty, the open heart for all goodness, the responsive mind, the tender heart, the aspiring soul—which go to make up fulness of life. Most people live a poor maimed life, as though they carried about one or other mortified limb, dead in itself and a burden to the body. But they do not realise that their minds are slow and their hearts heavy for want of the knowledge which is *life*.

**The Divine Method.**—We think, too, that the knowledge of divine things comes by feeling, and chide ourselves because we do not feel more. If we examine the teaching of Christ, we shall find that exceedingly little is said about feeling, and a great deal about knowing: that our Lord's teaching appeals, not to the heart, but to the intelligence. "Without a parable spake he not unto them." Why? That, "hearing they should not hear, and seeing they should not see, neither should they understand."

Here we have a method exactly contrary to all usual methods of teaching. In a general way, the teacher labours to make what he has to say plain to the dullest; and, indeed, we are impatient and fretful under poem or apologue, the meaning of which is not clear at the first glance. That is, we choose that all labour shall be on the part of the teacher, and none upon that of the learner.

Whatever we get in this way is soon lost—'lightly come, lightly go';—for knowledge is only to be had at the cost of labour of mind. As regards the knowledge of our religion, above all, we must read, and inwardly digest; for it is only upon that which we take into us as part of ourselves that we grow. Our Lord knew this, and delivered no easy sayings for the instruction of the people. Even his disciples did not understand. Let us put ourselves in their place, and listen to the Master's 'hard' sayings—hard intellectually as well as morally—and see what we should get out of them on the first hearing. The involved arguments of St Paul are infinitely plainer; the dark sayings of the prophets, the Apocalypse itself, are easier to understand, so far as their meaning is decipherable at all, than the simple-sounding sayings of Christ. But this very fact evidences our Lord's way of teaching us that life comes of knowledge, the knowledge of God.

**The Bible contains a Revelation of God.**— Where shall we find our material?—for we can only think as we are supplied with the material for thought. First and last, in the Bible; for the knowledge of God comes by revelation. We can only know Him as he declares and manifests Himself to us. There are, no doubt, 'few, faint, and feeble' rays of revelation in books held sacred by various eastern nations; and this we should expect, because God is the God of all flesh, and does not leave Himself without a witness anywhere; but feeble rays in an immense void of darkness are not accepted even by the people who possess them as affording a knowledge of God. They do not aim at or conceive of such a knowledge. They sit in darkness as they have sat from the beginning, and must needs sit until they receive the light of revelation.

**The Higher Criticism.**—A serious danger threatens us who hold the means of knowledge in what is called the higher criticism. It is no doubt well that scholars should give critical attention to every jot and tittle of the Scriptures; and the danger to us does *not* lie in any possibility that in the Bible we have no word of God, but merely the literature of the Hebrew nation. So soon as men's eyes turn from minute literary criticism to the gradual revelation of our God in His beauty (the progressive revelation which we get in the Bible alone), the truth of the Book is confirmed to us; and we *know*, without proof—

> "Thou canst not prove the Nameless,
> Nor canst thou prove the world thou movest in,
> For nothing worthy proving can be proven,
> Nor yet disproven."—[1]

Plato has said the last word on this matter for our day as well as his own. The danger I refer to is that, while occupying our minds about questions of criticism, we neglect the knowledge which cannot come without labour; that we forsake the earnest and devout study of the Bible, the one way of approach to the knowledge of God.

Already we begin to gather the fruits of our ignorance. Little books with Bible sayings, worked into specious arguments to prove a philosophy of life which the Bible does not sanction, come to us as a new and wonderful gospel. We talk of new developments of Christianity, when the Christianity of the Bible offers infinite scope for development in the beauty of holiness and in the knowledge of our illimitable God. We are offered on all hands religions about Christ and without Christ We are taught to believe that, "God manifest in the flesh," means no more than the divine in ourselves, and that every power that was used by Christ is available to us.

A smug religiosity is upon us, a religion of which we ourselves are the measure; whether we call it 'Christianity on a Higher Plane,' or Buddhism, or Theosophy; or whether, like the Dukhobors, we decline to obey human law, because we choose to believe ourselves under the immediate direction of

[1] *The Myths of Plato*, Professor Stewart.

God,—saying, with that poor little community in Lancashire, 'There is no law but God's law,' and drawing the absurd inference that all human law is transgression:—all these things have the one interpretation; we are declining from the knowledge of God.

**Indecision.**—In another way still we are eating the fruit of our ignorance. A paralysing hesitancy and uncertainty are upon us. We are tolerant of all beliefs because we have none. 'We do not know,' we say; 'we are not sure.' 'What right have we to think that the creed of another man, or another people, is not as true as ours?' The very newspapers ask us, Is Christianity effete?—and we presume to discuss the question; or, at any rate, we are able to listen in calmness while men toss to and fro the one question which is vital to us. Let us believe it—What think ye of Christ? Is the only question that matters. We cannot escape with the evasion, "We think not of Christ, but of the Father"—for the word is true, "No man cometh unto the Father but by me."

How are we to get this vital knowledge, without which we assuredly perish?—not in some unknown future state, but here and now, a slow paralysis creeps upon us. We have seen that there is but one source of illumination, the Bible itself. It is true that the divine Spirit is a light in every man's soul; but if a lamp is to be kindled, there must be the lamp; and it would seem as if the process followed by the Holy Spirit were to teach us by an arresting illumination, from time to time, of some phrase written in the Bible. Hence, our business is, before all things, to make ourselves acquainted with the text.

**Study of the Bible.**—How, then, shall we study

our Bible, bearing in mind that our aim is not textual criticism, or even textual knowledge, but the knowledge of God?

The interpreter is too much with us. We lean on him—whether in commentary, essay, sermon, poem, critique—and are content that he should think for us. It is better that we should, in the first place, try our own efforts at interpretation; when we fail or are puzzled is the time to compare our thought with that of others, choosing as interpreters men of devout mind and scholarly accomplishment. Orderly study, with the occasional help of a sound commentary, is to be recommended. To use 'good books,' by way of a spiritual stimulus, deadens in the end the healthy appetite for truth. The same remark applies to little text-books, with remarks meant to stimulate certain virtues or states of mind. The error that underlies these aids to private devotion (public worship is another matter) is, that their tendency is to magnify ourselves and our occasions, while they create in us little or no desire for the best knowledge. It is probable that even our lame efforts at reading with understanding are more profitable than the best instruction. The preparedness we need is of the mind and heart; we must pray to be delivered from prejudices and prepossessions, and wait upon God as the thirsty earth waits for rain.

In the Old Testament it is well, for example, to read a life through, with such breaks as may be convenient, remembering that there has been no such constraint upon the author as to make him a recording machine. He writes as he is, a man with ignorances which have not been informed, with prejudices which have not been corrected. You discern the man in his book, as any author is discerned in his writings. The difference in the Scriptures is that the men who wrote the Bible books were charged with the revelation of God and of His dealings with men; revelations of men also, discovered with a certain childlike simplicity which shows us to each other—as we surely appear to our Father—without excuse or extenuation, but with a strong appeal in our simplicity. Men are, we may believe, shown to us in the Bible as we each appear before God. Good men offend, are chastised and forgiven, even as children in a family.

Thus, for example, we all leave our homes to seek our fortune, even as Abraham did; but, with Abraham, the veil is lifted, and we are shown that God called him forth, led him on his way, put him through the slow discipline of a life, the results of which belonged to a time that came after. The Bible lives are typical; they disclose to us the inner meaning of our own. That restraining touch of God of which we are all aware, that inspiring whisper in the ear which comes to us at great moments, that fixing of the bounds of our habitation which is part of our Father's plan for each of us,—these things are presented in the lives of holy men of old.

**'Revelation' of the Bible Unique.**—Do not let us make a mistake. Because we find little hints in many books, hints of the Lord God, merciful and gracious, who will by no means clear the guilty, let us not run away with the idea that the peculiar revelation of the Bible is, in truth, a universal revelation. Every hint we get of the Being of God is derived, consciously or unconsciously, from the Bible, even as that of a candle is derived from the light of the sun. Does the freethinker, who knows no God, proclaim the love of man? No hint of the brotherhood and sonship of men has escaped into the world except through the revelation which God has vouchsafed to us through certain chosen men. Thoughts already revealed are made luminous to us by the light that is vouchsafed to each, but that is a quite different thing from the first inception of a revealing thought.

When we have mastered all the knowledge of God that has been progressively revealed in the Bible, then perhaps further revelation will be granted to men in the same gradual way.

**No Revelation is Repeated.**—It would appear, so far as we can discern the law, that God does not repeat a revelation which has been made; and, also, that as full a revelation as we are able to bear concerning our God has already been given, and recorded under divine authority. In this matter the present work of the Holy Spirit, who inspires, appears to be to illuminate a meaning here, another there, for each of us; so that our education in the knowledge of God is being gradually carried on, if we bring a hearing ear and an understanding heart.

In this way, our poets write and our painters paint under inspiration when they write and paint revealing truths. We may believe also, with the mediaeval Church, that a revelation is still going on of things not hitherto made known to men. Great secrets of nature, for example, would seem to be imparted to minds already prepared to receive them, as, for example, that of the 'ions' or 'electrons' of which that we call matter is said to consist. For this sort of knowledge also is of God, and is, I believe, a matter of revelation, given as the world is prepared to receive it.

But here the same two laws would appear to hold good. No revelation is repeated; the law of gravitation, the circulation of the blood, and the like, cannot twice be revealed to man; and, again, there is no overcrowding of such revelations. Not until we have mastered, digested and made our own, that which has already been presented, is a new revelation offered to us.

This, probably, is why the Bible is unique as containing original revelations of God. We know Him so little, we are so very far from attaining the Bible conception of the beauty and the goodness of our God, that we are not ready for more. Let us observe,—God's dealings with individuals in this matter of revelation would always seem to have reference to the world. No man is taught for himself alone; and that for which the world—as represented by its best and most thoughtful people—is unripe by reason of ignorance, that revelation is withheld until the world is prepared. Therefore, the instructed conscience does not allow us to give heed to the 'Lo, here!' and 'Lo, there!' continually sounding in our ears; and we are equally careful as to how we receive private interpretations of the Scriptures, which are put before us as having escaped the vigilance of the Church until to-day. In the matter of our great first duty, it behoves us to keep to 'sober walking in true gospel ways.'

**Interpretation.**—As for distinguishing between the merely human and the inspired elements in the Bible, the way to this is not by critical study and destructive criticism, but by a gradual absorption of the idea of God as it is unfolded to us through the long preparation of the Old Testament, the glorious manifestation of the Gospels, and the application to the life of the Church which we find in the Acts and the Epistles. By long, slow study and by quick heart's love we shall learn to discern God, to know in an instant those words which are not of him; to know that 'break their teeth in their jaws,' for instance, is no word of God, but an utterance of the violent human heart, allowed to pass without comment, as are most of the ways and words of men recorded in the Bible.

We shall be able, as a reward of long study, to distinguish when a popular legend crops up, by the signs that it contains no revelation of God, no simple portrayal of man. But we shall not venture to say, that, because a story is not the sort of incident we may meet with any day in the street, it is therefore not of divine inspiration. The narration of such an incident (and there are many of them in the Bible) is merely one of *accidental*, outside truth, with little illuminating value. How the *essential* truth may be revealed to us, whether by parable or record, we cannot say; but we know that we have all heard the tempting voice in the garden, have all eaten the fruit, have all become miserably aware of ourselves, and have left, though not without hope, the paradise of innocent souls. Nay, that very story of the stopping of the sun in its course, an embedded myth, let us say, is recorded, we may believe, by the inspiration of God. We have all had times in our lives when the sun has not been permitted to go down upon us until we have wrought a deliverance, escaped a peril, done a work. It would seem as if the divine Spirit taught essential truths, the truths by which we live, by all means fitted to the understanding of men. But let us be extremely chary as to how we use this method of interpretation. No doubt God instructed his people by figures; but also, no doubt, he instructed them by facts; and when the simple fact carries its own interpretation, let us beware how we seek for another.

**Sentimental Humanity.**—Of another thing also let us beware. We may not endeavour to interpret the Scriptures in the spirit of sentimental humanity preached as the highest gospel to-day. That thousands should fall in the wilderness because they murmured or because they rebelled; that the earth should open and swallow certain haughty chieftains; that the punishment of death should fall upon men for an act of irreverence—such records as these by no means disprove the truth of the Bible. There may be inaccuracies of statement; for verbal inspiration, the use of the writer as an amanuensis, would destroy the human element which appears to be essential in all the communications of God with men. But let us not be in a hurry to cry, 'Away with all such fables!'

When a ship goes down with all hands, when flood and fire destroy their thousands, when famine and pestilence are abroad, an older piety would have called it the visitation of God; and that is precisely what the Bible statements amount to. If we say, bad drainage, unhealthy conditions, carelessness, errors in construction, flood or storm, we only put in the intermediate step. These are offences for which God visits men; and wind and storm are still fulfilling his word.

The mystery is one we find in life as well as in the chronicles of the Old Testament. Our Lord throws some light upon it in his remarks about that

Galilean tower; but it is conceivable that the final answer may be that death is less momentous in the thought of God, who knows the hereafter, than to us, who are still in the dark. Christ wept, not for Lazarus: his sorrow was for the griefs that fall upon all men, as upon the two sisters. Perhaps He would have said, 'If they only knew!'

**Superstition.**—I have indicated some of the prejudices and misconceptions likely to obtrude themselves upon us in reading the Bible. These and such as these put away, we shall be prepared to read with open mind and willing heart, until we learn gradually the ways of God with men, and something of the divine purity, tenderness, love, and justice. If we are told that the story of the Flood, another tale like that of Joseph, laws like those of Moses, and much besides, appear in the records of nations that knew not God, here is no ground for surprise. God is the God of all flesh; and surely, there never was a nation with which he had no dealings. The distinction is in knowing. To the nation who knew God— and was favoured, on account of its peculiar spiritual insight, to transmit what it received to the rest of the world—was revealed something of the interpretation of those dealings of God with men about which the nations who knew not God were pathetically and cruelly in the dark. The mind that knows not God is of necessity a prey to superstition. Only the other day, in a plague-struck district of India, boxes containing stationery for a public examination came to hand. Soon the report was rife in the bazaar that plague was in the boxes, and that, as soon as the sahib opened them, he would let it loose in the town. Nay, did not Israel itself, for our warning, relapse into ignorance of God, and, like the nations, sacrifice its sons and daughters to Moloch—the people gave of the fruit of its body for the sins of its soul.

**An Indulgent God.**—An element of peril in the teaching of our day is the continual presentation of our God as an *indulgent* Parent; whereas the Bible presentation is of a Father "who chasteneth whom he loveth, and scourgeth every son whom he receiveth," and who most of all chastened and scourged the only begotten Son of whom he said, "This is my beloved Son, in whom I am well pleased." Undue solicitude about our own pains and grievances may well interfere with the educative purposes of God.

**Christ presented in the Gospels.**—The main object of the Gospels is to hold up for our regard a presentation of the image of Christ; therein we may see him as he walked among men, as he looked upon men, as he spake, as he worked, as he died. There is no personage of history whom we have the means of knowing so completely as we may know our Lord; and the object in our gospel reading should be, less to find words of comfort and admonition for ourselves, than to perceive with our minds and receive upon our hearts the impress of Christ. To know him is life, and is the whole of life; and every thought of Him, walking in the cornfields, sitting weary by the well, moving among crowds .or in solitary places, raising his eyes upon the multitude, taking by the hand that little maid,—every such living conception we get of Christ is life to us. Just as, from the apparently casual touches of the painter, the living likeness grows, so, by laying upon the canvas of our hearts every apparently casual and insignificant detail about our Master, we shall

by degrees gather a living vision of the Son of Man;
and dearer to us than any beauty on the earth or
in the heavens will become the thought—

> "Of Jesus, sitting by Samaria's well,
>   Or teaching some poor fishers on the shore."[1]

**Miracles.**—If we would see the vision, we must
keep the single eye, unclouded by the breath of many
words which wing from many mouths. Especially
are men clamorous to prove that 'miracles do not
happen,' except as it is within everyone's power
to do miracles for himself!

The mist of words upon this subject is very apt
to darken the mind; but, if we are careful to instruct our conscience on some two or three points,
we shall not be blinded by this mote of destructive
criticism. In the first place, perhaps miracles are
no such great things as we make of them. St John
calls those which he records not miracles, but signs.
It is possible that in our day we have, or might
have, the *substance*, the entire faith in Christ, which
does away with the need of signs. As for the in-
credibility of the Gospel miracles, so fit and precious
as evidences of the mind of Christ, all that scientists
can say against them is that such a circumstance
as the turning of water into wine, for example, has
not come within their experience. They can no
longer say that such acts are impossible, nor that
they are contrary to the laws of nature. The amazing
discoveries of recent years have made scientific men
modest; they perceive that they do not know the
laws of nature, and are only acquainted with a

[1] Trench's *Sonnets.*

few of the ways of nature; and therefore they know that nothing is impossible.

Again, people think they can effect a compromise. They think they can still believe in God and in Christ, may even call themselves Christians, and yet scoff at the possibility of miracles as at a notion belonging to a benighted age. But they lose sight of the proportion of faith. They fix their minds upon certain incidents, and lose sight of the fact that the Christian life is altogether of the nature of a miracle. That God should hold intercourse with man; that we may pray, knowing, with full assurance, that we are heard and shall be answered; that at our word the hearts of princes will surely be refrained; that the fit and right desires of our hearts will be fulfilled, though always in simple and seemingly natural ways—these things, which come to all of us as signs, are they not of the nature of miracles? Do they not imply the immediate and personal action of our God, not in your behalf or mine alone, but in behalf of each of the creatures of his infinite care?

**The Words of Christ.**—Next after the Death upon the Cross, the deepest amazement of the Gospel story is, not miracles, but words. "Never man spake like this man," said that servant of the Temple sent to apprehend Jesus; and it was given to him to declare the unique distinction of Christ. Dare any man stand up and offer himself to the world with such words as: "I am the bread of life," "I am the light of the world," "I am the truth," "Come unto me, all ye that are weary, and I will give you rest"? It is in verifying the truth of these and such like sayings of Christ that Christianity consists; and all Christians everywhere and at all times have *known* these things to be true, with the knowledge that comes of experience; and this is the knowledge which is life. When we begin to get this sort of knowledge, the miracles of Christ are important to us only as they manifest the mind of our Master, his kindness and his pity, the necessity that was upon him to do acts of mercy.

**The Incarnation and the Resurrection.—** Another tendency of thought in our day is to deny the Incarnation and the Resurrection of Christ, to suppose that He was born and died and remained in the grave as do other men; but that He was truly the best among men, and our great example. None are more ready than scientific men to admit their profound ignorance of the causes of birth and life and death. They know the usual processes exactly; but causes, principles, elude them. We are hemmed in by mysteries as much in the domain of science as in that of religion. No one is prepared to say that the Incarnation could not be, nor the Resurrection; but, if these things were not as they are described, then are we indeed, as St Paul says, without hope. Christ is not. For, if He were a man like other men, then, indeed, would the charge brought against him by the Jews have been correct; and, "This man blasphemeth," would deprive us of all inspiration from the life of Christ, from the peace of his death, and from the hope of his resurrection.

**Trivial Doubts.—**It is necessary that conscience should be instructed as to the grave issues of doubts that are lightly handled in magazine or newspaper, and in books to be found in most houses, because our first duty is not possible to us while we have a divided mind. The first commandment is, we are told, "Thou shalt love the Lord thy God with all thy heart, and with all thy soul, and with all thy mind, and with all thy strength." How can we love Him whom we do not know, and how can we know Him concerning whom we are not sure? And, also, let us remember at our peril, that a doubt once entertained remains with us, is incorporated with us, and we are liable to its appearance at any moment. It recurs, as certain bodily ailments recur when they are, as we say, in the blood. We are inclined to think that there is a certain distinction in doubt, that a sceptical turn is a sign of intellectual power. The activity of a lesser mind may be shown by doubting in things divine as in things human; but the greater mind takes in all the bearings of the point at issue, and the darkness of doubt disappears before a luminous understanding. It has been well said that, "To the living and affirmative mind difficulties and unintelligibilities are as dross, which successively rises to the surface, and dims the splendour of ascertained and perceived truth, but which is cast away, time after time, until the molten silver remains unsullied; but the negative mind is lead, and, when all its formations of dross are skimmed away, nothing remains."[1]

The instructed conscience would pronounce, 'Loyalty forbids,' when we would entertain thoughts derogatory to Christ, dishonouring to God; because only such a conscience perceives how much is implied in this or that sceptical idea; knows, too, that the edifice of our faith is no dead structure of opinions and doctrines, but is a living body, liable to bleed to death through a wound.

[1] Coventry Patmore.

The uninstructed conscience, on the contrary, is persuaded that 'Truth' is so all-important that it is our duty to consider, examine, and finally cherish every objection presented to the mind. It must be remembered that objections are negative and not affirmative; that Truth consists in affirmations and not in negations; that, the affirmation duly apprehended, the negation disappears as a cloud before the sun; that we have no right to tamper with the negations of doubt until we have got the assurance of knowledge.

# CHAPTER XV

## SOME INSTRUCTORS OF CONSCIENCE: NATURE, SCIENCE, ART

**Nature—The Debts of Recognition, Appreciation, and Preservation.**—Conscience must brace itself under the instruction of other teachers besides those I have named. People are beginning to know that it is a shameful ignorance to live in this rich and beautiful world and not know the things about us even by name. The inheritors of precious collections recognise it as a duty to know, and to know about, the things they own: not to do so would be boorish ignorance. Here is a duty that lies upon us all; for we all enter on the inheritance of the heavens and the earth, the flowers of the field and the birds of the air. These are things to which we have right, no one can take them from us; but, until we get as much as a nodding and naming acquaintance with the things of Nature, they are a cause rather of irritation and depression than of joy.

Let us believe it, ignorance is a vice that never goes unpunished, and,

"The loud laugh that speaks the vacant mind,"

startling us in the midst of a quiet scene of natural

beauty, speaks not only of vacuity, but of the resentment and soreness of ignorance. We owe debts to things as well as to persons—the debts of recognition, appreciation, and preservation.

**The Schooling of Nature.**—In this matter of instruction in the things of Nature, we owe yet more to ourselves: for,

> "Nature never did betray the heart that loved her";—

and, in return for our discriminating and loving observation, she gives us the joy of a beautiful and delightful intimacy, a thrill of pleasure in the greeting of every old friend in field or hedgerow or starry sky, of delightful excitement in making a new acquaintance.

But Nature does more than this for us. She gives us certain dispositions of mind which we can get from no other source, and it is through these right dispositions that we get life into focus, as it were; learn to distinguish between small matters and great, to see that we ourselves are not of very great importance, that the world is wide, that things are sweet, that people are sweet, too; that, indeed, we are compassed about by an atmosphere of sweetness, airs of heaven coming from our God. Of all this we become aware in "the silence and the calm of mute, insensate things." Our hearts are inclined to love and worship; and we become prepared by the quiet schooling of Nature to walk softly and do our duty towards man and towards God.

**In our Duty towards God.**—In the chief duty of man, his duty towards God, Nature is an exquisite instructor. We know the story of that young footman who, oppressed by his clumsiness, was brought to a sudden standstill when upon an errand by the contemplation of a leafless tree; the surprising wonder of the fact that the tree would presently break out into leaves arrested him. All the fitness and beauty of God's ordering of the world was presented to his mind. The leafless tree converted him; and, almost from the moment, he became eminent as a saint of God, beautiful for his humility and simplicity of life.

As sweet a teacher was that 'small moss' of whose ministration to him Mungo Park tells us:—

"I saw myself in the midst of a vast wilderness, in the depth of the rainy season—naked and alone, surrounded by savage animals, and men still more savage. I was five hundred miles from the nearest European settlement. All these circumstances crowded at once on my recollection, and I confess that my spirits began to fail me. . . . At this moment, painful as my reflections were the extraordinary beauty of a small moss in fructification irresistibly caught my eye. I mention this to show from what trifling circumstances the mind will sometimes derive consolation; for though the whole plant was not larger than the top of one of my fingers, I could not contemplate the delicate conformation of its roots, leaves, and capsula without admiration. Can that Being, thought I, who planted, watered, and brought to perfection, in this obscure part of the world, a thing which appears of so small importance, look with unconcern upon the situation and sufferings of creatures formed after His own image? Surely not! Reflections like these would not allow me to despair. I started up and, disregarding both hunger and fatigue, travelled forwards, assured that relief was at hand; and I was not disappointed."

**Nature teaches us Gratitude.**—But it is not only as she helps us in our own spiritual life that Nature instructs us in our duty to God. Some people have the grace to be tenderly and reverently thankful to the author of a great book, the painter of a great picture —thankful, if less reverently so, to the discoverer of a great invention. What daily and hourly thanks and praise, then, do we owe to the Maker and designer of the beauty, glory, and fitness above our heads and about our feet and surrounding us on every side! From the flower in the crannied wall to the glorious firmament on high, all the things of Nature proclaim without ceasing, "Great and marvellous are thy works, Lord God Almighty."

The advancement of Science in late years, and the preoccupation of men's minds with structural details of the various members of the natural world, have produced a thick mist to hide the Creator; and we have been content to receive the beauty that delights us and the fitness that astonishes us as self-produced and self-conceived. In this matter, Science has behaved like a child so much occupied with a new toy that to be reminded either of the maker or the giver of the toy is tiresome and vexatious. He does not deny either maker or giver, but the toy itself is all he cares about This state of preoccupation, which has, no doubt, done good service to the cause of knowledge, is passing by, and the scientific mind is becoming more and more aware of that higher Power than Nature herself which is behind all the workings of Nature.

With this recognition will come gratitude; and the thankful heart is the glad heart. Truly, a joyful and a pleasant thing it is to be thankful!

**Science.**—Science herself, whose business it is to discover to us what we call the laws of Nature, is a teacher upon whom the conscience, seeking for instruction, must wait sedulously. The rash conclusions and reckless statements of the person who has had no scientific training make him mischievous in society—a source of superstition and prejudice.

Scientific training is not the same thing as information about certain scientific subjects. No one in these days can escape random information about radium, wireless telegraphy, heredity, and much else; but windfalls of this sort do not train the mind in exact observation, impartial record, great and humble expectation, patience, reverence, and humility, the sense that any minute natural object enfolds immense secrets—laws after which we are still only feeling our way.

**Science distinguished from Information.—** This scientific attitude of mind should fit us to behave ourselves quietly, think justly, and walk humbly with our God. But we may not confound a glib knowledge of scientific text-books with the patient investigation carried on by ourselves of some one order of natural objects; and it is this sort of investigation, in one direction or another, that is due from each of us. We can only cover a mere inch of the field of Science, it is true; but the attitude of mind we get in our own little bit of work helps us to the understanding of what is being done elsewhere, and we no longer conduct ourselves in this world of wonders like a gaping rustic at a fair.

**Patient Observation.—**Let me again say that this is *due* from us, and is not a thing we may take up or leave alone as we think fit. Let each of us undertake the patient, unflagging, day-by-day observation of the behaviour of sparrow, spider, teazel, of clouds or winds, recording what we ourselves have seen, correcting our records as we learn to be more accurate, and being very chary of conclusions. All we find out may be old knowledge, and is most likely already recorded in books;

but, for us, it is new, our own discovery, our personal
knowledge, a little bit of the world's real work which
we have attempted and done. However little work
we do in this kind, we gain by it some of the power to
appreciate, not merely beauty, but fitness, adaptation,
processes. Reverence and awe grow upon us, and we
are brought into a truer relation with the Almighty
Worker.

**Art.**—A great promise has been given to the world
—that its teachers shall not any more be removed.
There are always those present with us whom God
whispers in the ear, through whom He sends a direct
message to the rest. Among these messengers are
the great painters who interpret to us some of the
meanings of life. To read their messages aright is
a thing due from us. But this, like other good
gifts, does not come by nature. It is the reward
of humble, patient study. It is not in a day or a
year that Fra Angelico will tell us of the beauty of
holiness, that Giotto will confide his interpretation
of the meaning of life, that Millet will tell us of the
simplicity and dignity that belong to labour on the
soil, that Rembrandt will show us the sweetness of
humanity in many a commonplace countenance.

The artist—

> "Reaching, that heaven might so replenish him,
>   Above and through his art,"—

has indispensable lessons to give us, whether he
convey them through the brush of the painter, the
vast parables of the architect, or through such another
cathedral built of sound as 'Abt Vogler' produced:
the outward and visible sign is of less moment than
the inward and spiritual grace.

**We must learn to Appreciate and Discriminate.**—That we may be in a condition to receive this grace of teaching from all great Art, we must learn to appreciate and to discriminate, to separate between the meretricious and the essential, between technique (the mere power of expression) and the thing to be expressed—though the thing be no more than the grace and majesty of a tree. Here, again, I would urge that appreciation is not a voluntary offering, but a debt we owe, and a debt we must acquire the means to pay by patient and humble study. In this, as in all the labours of the conscience seeking for instruction, we are enriched by our efforts; but self-culture should not be our object. Let us approach Art with the modest intention to pay a debt that we owe in learning to appreciate. So shall we escape the irritating ways of the connoisseur!

# CHAPTER XVI

## SOME INSTRUCTORS OF CONSCIENCE: SOCIOLOGY, SELF-KNOWLEDGE

**Sociology—How other People live.**—"With all thy getting, get understanding," says the wise man; and we are never too young or too much engaged with work or pleasure to escape the duty of understanding how other people live. What are their needs? What things will do them good, and what things will do them harm? It behoves us all to think about the housing of the poor, the drink question, the care of the sick, the best way of dealing with crimes and offences, the teaching of the ignorant, whether they be persons or nations.

"I was an hungered," says Christ, "and ye fed me; naked, and ye clothed me; sick and in prison, and ye visited me." Perhaps no words spoken by our Master have come home with more intensity of meaning to every Christian soul, and few of us escape the sense of self-condemnation; and this, not so much because we are hard-hearted, unfeeling, and without pity—indeed, it is quite otherwise—an appeal in the newspapers brings an overwhelming and injurious amount of help. A beggar in the street grows rich on pennies. Any 'case' that we hear of we are very eager to help, as much to satisfy our conscience, because of those words of Christ's, as for the sake of the sufferer.

**Conditions of Helpfulness.**—But these casual efforts of ours are the despair of people who go to work steadily and conscientiously to help their brothers who are in need. These tell us of the evils of promiscuous charity, so we make up our minds that it is best not to 'give' at all; we are likely to do more harm than good, and so we content ourselves with a few subscriptions to certain public charities. In this matter, as in so many others, we err through the lack of an instructed conscience. It behoves each of us to lay ourselves out for instruction, to read, inquire, think, to look about us for a way of acting, believing—

> That Circumstance, a sacred oracle,
> Speaks with the voice of God to faithful souls;

and it is usually *in our way,* and not by going out of our way, that we shall find the particular piece of brotherly work appointed for us to do.

But we must keep our eyes open: the right thing is never obtrusive, and we may pass it by without observation. We must bear three things in mind. We must get a wide care and knowledge concerning the needs of men; we must devote ourselves, with understanding, to some particular effort for the needy; and, in all our endeavours, we must bear in mind our Master's way: What *wouldst thou* that I should do unto thee? he asked; and let us believe that charitable efforts, which go against the grain of the persons benefited, miss that principle of love which alone gives us a right to do service to others. It is particularly needful to bear this in mind in days when it is rather difficult to reach individuals, and we have to do our work through organisations. But organisations fail continually because they overlook this guiding principle, 'What wouldst thou?' It is not only self-relieving effort that is due from us, but discriminating and considerate love.

**To know Ourselves is Wisdom.**—It is difficult to find a name which covers what we are and what we may become, but let us call it philosophy; for to know ourselves is wisdom. We all like to get what we call knowledge of ourselves from phrenologists, readers of handwriting, and the like, and from the polite sayings of our acquaintances. But this is the knowledge that puffeth up, because it is usually flattering and, therefore, false. We may deserve praise for the thing we are praised for; but flattery fills us with the notion that we are made up of this or the other charming quality, and that those of our friends who see another side are unkind and unjust.

This is so plain to some people that they think the best plan is to leave self alone altogether, never thinking at all about what is in them, whether for good or ill, unless perhaps they are brought to book for some grave fault. Their course would be right enough if living were the easy, casual thing they make of it. But to be born a human being is to come into possession of a great estate—forest land here, copses there, cornfields, meadows, fisheries, what not: indeed, more than an estate, as I said before—a kingdom, the kingdom of Mansoul.

**Self-Knowledge Impersonal.**—Here, as in other estates, the casual proprietor ruins his land; field after field runs to waste and to weeds, and the land is hardly to be 'cleaned' in a generation.

All the same, it is a mistake to think about ourselves personally. Our Lord has said once, for all time, "If I bear witness of myself, my witness is not true." It is a wonderful saying, true even for our Master—how much more for us! We generally have too much taste to bear witness of ourselves out loud —to tell other people how plucky and generous, how clever or how sweet we are; but do we never bear witness to ourselves of ourselves—privately plume ourselves upon this or that good quality or fine action? When we do so, *our witness is not true*: the virtue for which we praise ourselves to ourselves is a virtue we do not possess. The fine action we admire ourselves for has ceased to be fine; our own praise of it has taken out all the virtue.

**Greatness of Human Nature.**—This would appear to prove them in the right who say it is best not to think of ourselves at all; but, *ourselves* may mean two things,—our own little sayings, doings and feelings—poor things at the best—or that glorious human nature, with its unmeasured capacities, which we share with heroes and sages, with Christ himself.

It is profanity to say of greed, sloth, sin, depravity of every kind, 'Oh, it's human nature'; for human nature is fitted for all godlike uses, and the Son of Man came to show us all that we may be when we do not reject the indwelling of our God. It is only as we realise the greatness of human nature that we understand what our Lord means when He says that one soul is worth more than the whole world. His words are always spoken in truth and soberness, and this is no fantastic valuation; nor does it mean, I think, that every single soul is so valuable to God; but that every single soul or person is so immeasurably great in itself; and this is the reason of the infinite divine solicitude that not one should perish. Therefore let us take stock, not of what is peculiar to us as individuals, but what is proper to each of us as human beings, remembering that we have no true ownership of the wealth of which we are ignorant.

Also, it is only a sense of the greatness of the poorest human soul that will awaken in us the passionate brotherhood which should help each of us to do our little share of the saving of the world; for we are called upon to work with our Master as well as for him. The object of this little book is to introduce to themselves any who are not yet acquainted with their own worth; so I need not here go over the reasons why, or the manner in which, we should know ourselves. Only one thing I should like to say on this point. Let us not put this sort of knowledge away from us as too troublesome and as making us too responsible. We have simply to know in the first place; and are not bound to be labouring all the time to feed imagination, exercise reason, instruct conscience, and the rest. In this sphere of self-knowledge, as in so much else, set things going, and they go;—

"Begin it, and the thing will be completed."

We are so mercifully made that the ordering of ourselves becomes unconscious to those of us who take it as a duty; it is the casual people who land in bogs or are brought up against stone walls.

# *THE FUNCTION OF CONSCIENCE*

## CHAPTER XVII

### CONVICTION OF SIN

**Convicts of Sin.**—Conscience would seem to have but a single office—to convince us of sin—that is, of transgression. The older divines used to speak much of an approving conscience; but this approval would appear to be no more than silence; for self-approbation, as we have seen, is, in itself, an offence. Then, when conscience says nothing we are all right? You ask. By no means, for the verdict of conscience depends upon what we know and what we habitually allow.

We gather from the reports of travellers among uncivilised tribes that the consciences of all men forbid them to murder, to steal, slander, dishonour their parents, and commit certain other offences. The consciences of all require them to be hospitable to strangers and faithful to friends, and in even the most debased there would seem to be a sense of the honour and worship due to God, however low a conception they may form of the divine. Even the baby, not able to run, knows that it is 'naughty' to disobey.

Each of us has a mentor within to condemn his misdeeds; but the judge of our bosom gives his verdict only upon the errors he knows; and conscience waits, as we have seen, for instruction in many directions.

**Ignorance.**—Not even religion is a substitute for the instructed conscience, any more than the love of God would teach an ignorant man to read. Conscience is given to us, but the due instruction of this power we must get for ourselves. It is very important to bear this in mind in our reading of history, in our judgment of current events, of public and of private persons; above all, in our judgment as to what we may and may not do and think ourselves.

This reflection, again, gives us a certain power of moral adjustment. We do not seek to justify hard things said or done by a good man; we perceive that on that point the good man's conscience has not been informed: we do not reverse our judgment of him and say, 'He is a bad man,' for this or that offence against gentleness or justice, but, 'He has done wrong in this, because he has not taken pains to inform himself.' Realising how liable the best and wisest are to err through moral ignorance, we are careful to keep ourselves open to instruction.

**Allowance.**—Not only may ignorance limit the action of conscience, but allowance may blind this inner judge. When we see offences in others, and do not call them by their right name; when we allow ourselves habitually to do that we ought not to do, or to think that we ought not to think, conscience stops speaking, as it were, and no longer testifies against the wrong.

**Prejudice.**—One more way of stultifying conscience we must watch against with jealous care, because this is an offence which has the appearance of righteousness: I mean the absorption of the mind by a single idea. Most wars and all persecutions, family quarrels, jealousies, envyings, resentment against friends, half the discords and unhappinesses of life, may be traced to this cause. The danger is, that good people may so fix their eyes upon one point of offence that they lose the sense of proportion. A spot the size of a penny piece hides the sun.

Bearing in mind that either ignorance, allowance, or prejudice makes conscience of little avail to its owner, we are not dismayed by even so appalling a vision of the Church in Alexandria as Kingsley gives us in *Hypatia*. Christianity itself does not suffer in our eyes. We perceive that the monks of Nitria, with Cyril at their head, sinned through moral ignorance, through the hardness that comes of allowance, and the madness wrought by a besetting idea; and that, through a conscience full of offence, they put shame on the Christianity they professed.

Considering these things, we do not miss the lessons of history, or of life, through the strife of contrary opinions about good men and great movements. We perceive the moral blind spot which might have been enlightened in many a great leader (and still we know him to be great and good); we discern the danger of the besetting idea in many a popular movement which is yet an advance.

There are few things more cheering to the student of history than the sense that the consciences of men and nations are under continually increasing enlightenment. From age to age and from year to year we become aware of more delicate offences, more subtle debts, because our God is dealing with us and instructing us; and the reward of men and nations who seek for that wisdom which cometh from above is a continual advance in moral enlightenment, an ever greater power of seeing the right in small things and great.

**Sin.**—"Conscience doth make cowards of us all," he said, who knew what was in men better than any save One. We put a gloss on the saying, and lose its force. We read: Conscience makes cowards of all wrong-doers; or, of us all, when we have done wrong, and, behold, a loophole through which we escape condemnation on most days in the year. We hear it stated that the sense of sin is no longer a general experience, that people can no longer confess with conviction that they "have left undone those things which they ought to have done, and done those things which they ought not to have done." In so far as this is true, it is because conscience is drugged or beguiled.

**Uneasiness of Conscience.**—That conscience makes us all cowards is still a luminous truth. We wake up in the morning with a sense of fear, un-easiness, anxiety—causeless, so far as we know, but there it is—the horrid fear that something is going to happen to us because we deserve it. 'Nerves,' says the man of science: very likely, though the hale and hearty know this fear as truly as do the ailing. But to say 'nerves,' or 'hypochondria,' or 'the blues,' or the older 'megrims,' or 'vapours,' is only to name a symptom and not a cause. The cowardice of conscience drives us all, old and young, rich and poor, whether into what we call nervous ailments, or into the mad and lusty pursuit of business or pleasure. Either of these we know for a soporific, carrying us through the day, passing the time, as we say; and, if we only get tired enough, bringing sleep at night. But the busiest and gayest lives have their moments of blank fear when the terrors of conscience are sprung upon them. Men call reason to their aid. There is nothing in their lives of which they can convict themselves; they live as other men do, kindly, respectable, even religious lives. Why should they fear conscience? Why, indeed?

**Sins of Omission.**—At such moments that accusation, from which there is no escape, comes with startling force to the memory,—"I was an hungered, and ye fed me not," with those other charges summing up the casual omissions which seem to us at such moments to be the whole history of our lives. How can we ever overtake the little things we have not done? We are cast into the outer darkness of dismay, and are cowards, each of us, before his conscience. In a general way, we are content to confound sin with crime. Because we have not been guilty of lying or theft or any of the sins against society which the law punishes, we are like that young ruler, and say of the commandments, 'All these have I kept from my youth up.' Then, like him, we are shown the things we might do, and might have done, and go forth ashamed—aware of sin.

'There is no health in us,' we cry, with the sincerity of a broken heart; 'I am such a poor thing,' or, 'such a worthless fellow'; or, 'So foolish was I and ignorant, I was as a beast before Thee.' Such as these are the cries of the unsophisticated conscience, as it catches a glimpse, now and again, of the vastness of life, of the ten or ten thousand talents which it implies.

'Who is sufficient for these things?' And there is no rest for the uneasy conscience until we can say, 'My sufficiency is of God.'

**The Chiding of Conscience.**—It is the office, we are told, of the Holy Spirit to convince the world of sin, of righteousness, and of judgment; and, in the constant operation of the divine Spirit upon the spirits of men, we find the secret of how we become aware of sin when we have done nothing in particular to be ashamed of; how we crave after a righteousness greater than we know; and how the sense of a present judgment, to come upon us to-day or to-morrow, awakens with us many a morning and goes to bed with us many a night when no particular wrong-doing comes home to convict us.

Because these convictions are of God, we do not drive them away in the multiplicity of interests and amusements; neither do we sit down and pity ourselves, and encourage what are called nervous maladies. There is a more excellent way.

But when we count up our blessings, let us not fail to number this, of the continual chiding of conscience. A wise man has said that, were there no other evidence of the existence of God, the conscience of man is a final proof. Let us accept the strivings of conscience in this light, and rejoice.

# CHAPTER XVIII

## TEMPTATION

**Sudden Temptation.**—Though in placid moments they are what we are most aware of, our sins of omission are by no means the greatest trouble of our lives. Like St Christopher, we have to fight our way against the floods, however quiet our lives may seem. Some little peevishness or petulance about a trifle, some slight resentment against a friend, some entanglement in our circumstances,—and it is as though, like the cuttlefish, we had darkened all the waters about us. Suddenly, without an instant's warning, we are in a flood of rage, resentment, crooked contrivings, perhaps unclean imaginings. We are swept off our feet and cannot recover ourselves. We flounder and beat the waves, long and wearily, before we win our way back to righteousness and peace. We do not intend, will, or foresee these sudden falls; we become as persons possessed, and have no power in ourselves to struggle out of the flood of malice, pride, uncleanness, greed, envy, or whatever else of evil has overwhelmed us.

The fact that we have not foreseen these falls, points to a cause outside ourselves—to those powers and principalities in high places, whose struggle for dominion over us the Bible reveals; and the revelation is confirmed by our own sad and familiar experience.

**Temptation comes from without and from within.**—This is Temptation, reaching us sometimes plainly from without, but more often, it would seem, through the movement of some spirit of evil which has access to our own spirit. If we say there is no Holy Spirit, and no evil spirit, and no spirit of a man, —if, like the Sadducees of old and their kind to-day, we do not believe in any such thing—there is nothing more to be said. But if we are aware of the movements of our own spiritual life, and observant of that life in those about us, if we have taken cognisance of how good and evil come as a flood upon the world or upon an individual soul, we shall recognise that there is a source of temptation outside of ourselves, even as there is a source of strength and blessedness. We shall know that 'we wrestle not with flesh and blood,' but with spiritual wickedness in high places; and we shall lay ourselves out to understand the laws and conditions of temptation, and shall look eagerly for ways of escape.

Literature is full of tales of temptation, yielded to, struggled against, conquered. Sometimes temptation finds us ready and there is no struggle, as in the case of Tito Melema;[1] sometimes there is a struggle, as in that of Maggie Tulliver;[2] sometimes, a victory like that of Joseph.

It is in the Bible we find the most intimate records of temptations. We wonder to this day how Peter could, upon a sudden temptation, deny his Lord; how Judas should, after slow gathering of fretful and impatient thoughts, betray Him; how the disciples

---

[1] *Romola.*    [2] *The Mill on the Floss.*

should, in a sudden panic of fear, forsake Him and flee. And, when we think of falls like these, we ask ourselves the awful question, 'Lord, is it I?' 'Should I have done the like in his place?'

The very records of crimes and offences in the newspapers bring us the same awful fear; with like temptation, and in like conditions, perhaps we should have done the like.

A sense of the inevitableness of temptation, the nearness of sin, comes upon us, now and then, like a terror; and it is well we should realise that temptation is a fact of life—a fact to be faced; and, also, that we are besieged in our weak places, tempted always to those sins we have a mind to.

It is good and comforting to be assured, "There hath no temptation taken you but such as is common to men." It is good to know that, "He will with the temptation make a way of escape that ye may be able to bear it"; that, "Blessed is the man that endureth temptation"; that, "Resist the devil, and he will flee from you."

**Enter not into Temptation.**—But it is to our Master, "who was in all points tempted like as we are, yet without sin," that we go for the key of the whole matter. Because he knows what is in man, he has said to us," See that ye enter not into temptation."

This is the secret of heroic lives whose conflict is with circumstances and not with temptations: they do not *enter* into temptation. All our Lord's sayings come out of profound knowledge of the ways of the minds of men. He knew that an idea, an imagination, of envy or resentment, for example, once entertained, dallied with, takes possession of the mind; we cannot get rid of it, and we are hurried into action or speech upon that notion before ever we are aware. Here we have the line between temptation and sin. That an offensive idea should be presented, is not of ourselves and is not sin. But, once we open the gates of our thought to let in the notion, why, we may conquer in the end, through the grace of Christ our Saviour, and after conflict, tears, and sore distress. But such a fight against temptation is a terror to the Christian soul. Upon this battlefield, he who fights and runs away lives to fight another day.

**The Training of a Trusty Spirit.**—Blessed are the souls that endure temptation from without; who endure grinding poverty without hardness or greed, uncongenial tempers without bitterness, contrary circumstances without petulance; who possess their souls in patience when all things are against them: these are temptations from which we cannot escape, and which are part of the education of a trusty spirit. But this education is accomplished by resisting the temptations that reach us from within—the offences in thought suggested by trying circumstances. For, let us not make a mistake, all sin, even all crime, is accomplished in thought. Word and act are but the fruit of which the received and permitted thought is the seed. The battle of life for each of us lies in the continual repetition of what seems a most trifling act—the rejection of certain thoughts which present themselves at the very moment when they come. This is how we shall keep our soul as a fortress; and therefore our Master, who is aware of us, who knows how the evil thought, once admitted, floods the soul and darkens the eye, bids us pray, day by day: "Our Father, which art in Heaven, lead us not into temptation, but deliver us from evil; for thine is the kingdom, the power, and the glory, for ever and ever. Amen.'

We have a Father who cares and knows. We have a Saviour who saves his people *from their sins*. We are not left to ourselves; we have a King who governs us, whose power upholds us, and whom we glorify by every little effort of ours not to enter into temptation.

The way in the beginning is quite easy, before we *enter*, that is; we turn away our thoughts from beholding evil, the evil in another or the evil suggestion to ourselves; and we do so, not by reasoning the matter out, but just by thinking of something else, some other pleasant or interesting thing belonging for the moment to our lives. For we are so made that there is always with the temptation an easy and natural way of escape. It is well we should realise this, because, in things of the spirit, it is quite true that God helps those who help themselves; and, if we pray, "Lead us not into temptation," and do not take the simple provided way of escape by thinking of some other thing, we are asking to be treated as the men on a chessboard, and not as beings free to do as they will; who honour God by *willing* to flee from temptation; who stretch out a hand for help to Him who saves us.

**Penitence, Repentance, Restitution.**—Many a life is spoiled by what the Church at one time set forth as a chief Christian grace. The penitent is a distressful figure in early Church history. Days, months, a life, of self-mortification, were appointed to the repentant sinner. Where there is no Church discipline of the sort, men and women of a sorrowful spirit go about, living in penitence

for offences of the past or the present. We all
know the people who will not forgive themselves,
who weep and afflict themselves because they are
guilty of some discovered wrong in word or deed,
and they believe that this sorrowful gloom of theirs
is due to God and man because of their offence.

**The Forgiveness of Sins.**—And yet these very
people recite regularly, "I believe in the forgiveness
of sins." They do not understand that forgiveness
means instant, immediate, complete restoration to
the joy of God's favour; that the forgiveness of
Christian hearts is equally prompt, or it is not
forgiveness; and that there are no tears to be shed,
no dark remembrances to be cherished, after the one
sore and sorrowful confession, made with many tears,
"Father, I have sinned." Then, we hold up our
heads as free men, and no longer drag the prisoner's
chain. We repent—yes; that is, we turn away from
the sin, we enter not into the temptation, we keep fast
hold of the grace of our God; and we restore: "If
I have taken anything from any man, I restore him
fourfold": fourfold love and gentleness and service the
repentant soul brings to God and his brother; but
this is because he is glad: out of the joy of his heart
there is nothing he cannot do; and, above all, he will
away with the proud and sullen tears and regrets of
so-called penitence. Let that story of the Father who
ran to meet his returning prodigal, who received him
with honour and feasting, who fell upon his neck,—
image too tender for a man to have dared to conceive
it, but which is given us with the authority of Christ,—
let this amazing picture of the dealings of our God
be with us always to light up the dark places in our
own lives.

# CHAPTER XIX

## DUTY AND LAW

**Right and Wrong.**—Sin, temptation, repentance, throw us back upon something behind them all. Why is it wrong to do wrong? And, what is wrong? People have answered these questions in various ways. Some say it is wrong to neglect or offend other men, and that therefore to care for and consider our fellows is right; and right only because they choose to do it. Others say they have the right to do as they like: therefore they can do no wrong; but when other people injure them, these are ready enough to complain of suffering wrong. Others, again, say that whatever is natural is right; and on this ground they will justify greed, sloth, uncleanness, selfishness, saying, 'Oh, it's human nature.' By the way, let me again say, it is a grievous misrepresentation to put down what is low, lazy, and unworthy to human nature, and never to say of heroism, self-denial, devotion, these are human nature too. For, indeed, what human nature is depends upon how we use it. This nature of ours is capable of base behaviour, as we know too well; but it is equally capable of magnanimity and generosity. But people usually mean the poor side of human nature when they say that what is natural is right

**We all know the Law.**—These various gropings in the dark to find out the meaning and reasons of right and wrong are forms of self-deception.

*We all know* that sin is the transgression of the law. Every living soul is aware that there is a law. He is not able to put it into words, perhaps, and may make wild and dreadful errors in interpreting the law, but he is aware. The most ignorant savage knows as well as the Psalmist that, "Thy commandment is exceeding broad." But, because he is ignorant and base, he does not know that the law is beautiful and works for blessedness; that is, he has not an instructed conscience, but only a conscience dimly aware of a law, the meaning of which he gropes after in the dark.

He knows, too, that obedience to the undeciphered law is due from him. He is dimly conscious that law is everywhere; that—

> Or act or say, or do but think a thought,
> And such and such shall surely come to pass,
> Fore-ordered sequent of such act or thought.

His uneasiness is appalling; he tries to appease his conscience by sacrifice; to explain the riddle of life by superstitions, making his god such an one as himself.

Contrast this restless uneasiness in the dark with the serenity of the enlightened Christian conscience. The Christian, too, is aware of the law which is about him, closer than the air he breathes, ordering his relations with all persons and all things, ordering his affections and his thoughts. But the law does not irk him. "Oh, how I love thy law!" he cries with the Psalmist; and he takes up gladly his share of the work of the world, so much of the fulfilling of the law as is *due* from him; he acknowledges his *Duty*.

As the planets revolve round the sun in obedience to their law, so he revolves in the orbit of his life, and his deepest joy is Duty. Not that he fulfils the law which is within his heart. Like the planet on which he lives, he is constantly pulling away from the law he owns; but he is as continually recovered, so that he does indeed finish his course.

**Law and Will.**—The reason why it is a joy to perceive the law, and an unspeakable gladness to fulfil even a little of that law, is, that we recognise law as the expression of the perfect will of God. Law, existing by itself and for itself, without any to will or desire, is a monstrous thought—a thought to chafe our spirits and take the heart out of all our strivings—because there is no comfort of love in it and no reasonable conviction. But how good and pleasant it is to know that at the heart of all things is our God, who wills the good and right behaviour of every creature in His universe, and who enables us all for right doing, for that fulfilling of His law in which all things work together for good! Our little lives are no longer small and poor when we think of the great things of the world. They are a necessary part of the great whole, ordered under law, fulfilling His will, and singing as the morning stars in the gladness of obedience.

**Acquiescence.**—The possibility of an erratic course, of breaking away into space—a glittering object, may be, for a time; to be, by and by, quenched in darkness—should make us the more fervent in our duty-doing. All sense of bondage ceases when we say, "I rejoice to do thy will, O my God; yea, thy law is within my heart." And, with this spring of glad obedience within us, we arise and shine, because every feeble, faltering step is sustained; when we fall we are raised, when we pause we are strengthened and cheered to go on; and, poor things as we know ourselves to be, our path is that of the just, shining more and more unto the perfect day.

> "Stern Daughter of the Voice of God!
>    O Duty! if that name thou love,
> Who art a light to guide, a rod
>    To check the erring, and reprove;
> Thou, who art victory and law
> Where empty terrors overawe;
> From vain temptations dost set free;
> And calm'st the weary strife of frail humanity!
>
> "Through no disturbance of my soul,
>    Or strong compunction in me wrought,
> I supplicate for thy control;
>    But in the quietness of thought.
> Me this unchartered freedom tires,
> I feel the weight of chance desires;
> My hopes no more must change their name,
> I long for a repose that ever is the same.
>
> "Stern Lawgiver! yet thou dost wear
>    The Godhead's most benignant grace;
> Nor know we anything so fair
>    As is the smile upon thy face:
> Flowers laugh before thee on their beds,
> And fragrance in thy footing treads;
> Thou dost preserve the stars from wrong,
> And the most ancient heavens, through thee, are fresh
>    and strong.

"To humbler functions, awful Power,
    I call thee: I myself commend
Unto thy guidance from this hour;
    O let my weakness have an end!
Give unto me, made lowly wise,
The spirit of self-sacrifice;
The confidence of reason give;
And in the light of truth thy bondman let me live!"

WORDSWORTH.

# PART II

# THE WILL

## CHAPTER I

### THE WILL-LESS LIFE

IT perhaps occurs to the reader that man is indeed the Sphinx's riddle, and that the more we think of ourselves the more we are baffled. This is true enough; but the inference—'let the puzzle alone'— is by no means safe. For this baffling problem of human nature must needs occupy us from the cradle to the grave. It is that of which we have to render account, whose content is, those talents, the use of which is our business in life.

**Anarchy in Mansoul.**—So far as we have considered the matter, Heart, with its affections of Love and Justice, Intellect, with its Reason and Imagination, even Conscience itself, behave pretty much as do the several organs of the body—brain, lungs, heart, and so on; give them proper food, exercise, rest, and air, and they do their work of themselves. It hardly seems to be *we* who imagine or who love. We may not all be *consciously* dominated by ideas; but every writer knows how he 'reels off' almost without intention. Everyone knows how the affections behave, how love, as lord of the bosom, plays unaccountable and vexatious pranks, and commonly gives the poor man a sorry time. The blind god with his mischievous tricks is more than a pretty fancy; it is a symbol which presents very truly the whimsical behaviour of love when left to itself.

Conscience, too, for all the dignity and sobriety we attach to his name, is, left to himself, as whimsical and aggravating as any blind god. We know the persons of morbid conscience who are fussy over some ridiculous bit of 'packthread,' leaving their real relations and duties out of count.

Think, too, how heated and morbid the imagination becomes that is always feeding (commonly on poor trash), never working, never resting, and never coming into the fresh air of common day! We know the distorted views, sickly principles, and weak behaviour of the person who lets his imagination run away with him as a horse that has bolted runs away with his rider. Perhaps he takes to drugs, or drink, or trashy novels, to stimulate the tired jade; for go he must—he knows no other life. With a *menage* full of unbroken horses, each minded to go his own way and each able to drag the poor man after him, what is he to do? Who is able to order his affairs?

Mansoul is saved from anarchy by the Will, that power within us which, we know not how, has the ordering of the rest

**An Easy Life.**—It has been said that the Will is 'the sole practical faculty of man,' and we recognise this in our common speech. Whatever is done with the consent of the will we describe as *voluntary*; what is done without that consent is *involuntary*: and, as we have seen, we can reason, imagine, love, judge, without any action of the will. Indeed, life is made so easy for us, by conventions and class customs, that many poor souls live to man's estate, die in old age, and have never called upon Will to decide between this and that. They think as other people think, act as others act, feel what is commonly felt, and never fall back upon their true selves, wherein Will must act. Such lives are easy enough, but they are stunted and stinted in all directions. No power has been nourished and exercised or brought under the broad sky of God's dealings. Life is to such persons a series of casualties; things happen well or they happen ill, but they always *happen*; and the absence of purpose and resolution in themselves makes it impossible for them to understand that these exist in God; so their religion, also, comes to consist of conventional phrases and superstitions.

This is the most common development of the will-less life, marked by a general inanition of powers and an absence of purpose,—beyond that of being as others are, and doing as others do. The inmate of the mad-house, who reasons with amazing cunning, has his affections and his conscience too (did not Mr Dick make a valiant fight against that head of Charles I.?); but he is commonly lost for the want of will-power to order the inmates of his house of mind and his house of heart. So of the young man, who is nobody's enemy but his own, who is carried off his feet by every stray suggestion of pleasure or excitement.

It is well we should face the possibility of living without the exercise of will, in order that we may *will* and make our choice. Shall we live this aimless, drifting life, or shall we take upon us the responsibility of our lives, and *will* as we go?

# CHAPTER II

## WILL AND WILFULNESS

**Wilful Persons are of Various Dispositions.—**
What of the person who always contrives to get his
own way, whether he get it by means of stormy
scenes, crafty management, sly evasion, or dogged
persistence? The dogged and the blustering person
are commonly supposed to have strong wills; the sly,
and the managing person keep somehow out of our
notice, we do not make up our minds about them.
As a matter of fact, persons of these four classes may
get each their own way, with as little action of the
Will as is exercised by the casual person who lets
things slide. When we have given ourselves to Greed
or Vanity, Ambition or Lust, we pursue our way
without restraint from Will, and get what we want by
straight or devious ways, according to our nature.
The robber baron of the Middle Ages, a turbulent
man, without ruth or fear, whose action was commonly
the outcome of stormy passions,—he and his like are
supposed to be persons of strong will. Such a man
was the Wild Boar of the Ardennes,[1] such another,
Charles of Burgundy,[2] and such another, indeed, our
own reckless Coeur de Lion.[3] These heroes of the

[1] *Quintin Durward*, Scott.    [2] *Anne of Geierstein*, Scott

[3] *The Talisman*, Scott.

'strong will' are not without their qualities; they are generous and lavish, as ready to give as to take; and they will always have a following of the sort whose instinct it is to 'follow my leader.' The persons who compass their way by more subtle means are less attractive. King John[1] and Becky Sharp[2] do not win a following; we prefer Joab to Achitophel; and Esau is a more winning person than Jacob.

In the last two, we get the contrast we want, between the man of Will and the creature of Wilfulness. This contrast is not, as it would seem at first, between the man who pursues his desires above board and generously, and his brother who wins his way, sometimes by prudence and sometimes by craft. The difference lies deeper.

**The Wilful Person has one Aim.**—The wilful person is at the mercy of his appetites and his chance desires. Esau must needs have that red pottage, he must needs hunt, or marry, or do whatever his desires move him towards at the moment. So must needs do the crafty gambler, the secret drunkard, the slothful soul, the inordinate novel-reader, the person for whom 'life' means 'pleasure.' Each of these is steady to only one thing, he must always have his way; but his way is a will-o'-the-wisp which leads him in many directions. Wherever gratification is to be found—for his vanity, his love of nice eating, his desire for gay company, or his ambition, his determination to be first,—there he goes. He is a wilful man, without power or desire to control the lead of his nature, having no end in view beyond the gratification of some one natural desire, appetite, or affection. Mr Barrie's Sentimental Tommy is a valuable study

[1] Shakespeare.  [2] *Vanity Fair*, Thackeray.

of a wilful person. Tommy always attained his end, always found out a 'wy'; and his ends were often good enough in themselves. But Tommy is an ingrained *poseur*: he does many generous things, and is a bit of a genius; but all his efforts are prompted by the chance desires of his vanity. He must, at all hazards, impress an audience. He always gets his 'wy,' yet his life falls to pieces in the end because he is not dominated by Will, but by vanity.

Jacob, too, gets his way, often by subtle means, and every subtlety brings its chastisement; but he does not seek his way for its own sake. All his chance desires are subordinated to an end—in his case, the great end of founding the kingdom of promise. The means he uses are bad and good. "Few and evil are the days of my life," he complains at the end, so sore have been his chastisements; but, always, he has willed steadily towards an end outside of himself.

The career of the late Lord Beaconsfield is an interesting study, as showing the two phases of Wilfulness and Will. To begin with, he has only the rather dazzling wilfulness of a young man's ambition; he *will* shine, he *will* make himself heard in the House; and he does it. But there is nothing more; and the country feels him to be a creature of chance desires. But by and by Will manifests itself, the will of the great statesman. Personal desires are subjugated or disappear in the presence of the ruling will, and we get a man fit for the service of his country. We have no record of an era of wilfulness in Wellington; his was ever the iron will, iron to keep down not only those under him, but any turbulence of his own flesh or spirit. The 'Iron Chancellor' of

Germany had this same steadfastness of will, always accomplishing towards an end.

**A Brilliant Career does not demand Exercise of Will.**—But it is even possible to make the world wonder without an exercise of Will. Napoleon, who came upon Europe as a portent, was but impelled along the lines of least resistance in his nature—his genius, high courage, vanity, and inordinate ambition, —but he never reached the elevation of a man with an impersonal aim. He willed nothing outside himself. He had the lavish generosity of a child, and a child's petulant wilfulness; a child's instability, too, or how could he have borne the shame of retreating from Russia in advance of his army?

It is not safe to take success in life as a criterion. His Will is the measure of the man; and many a man has become rich or famous without willing, on the easy lines of his nature, by the strength of his desires; while many another of constant will lives unknown: and yet it is the persons of constant will, which implies impersonal aims, who are the world's great possession, and are discerned to be such.

We distinguish, for example, between rich, successful men. There are those who are simply accepted as rich; and there are those—merchants, manufacturers, shopkeepers, it matters little what—who have become rich and successful by accident, as it were; these are not the things they have willed; but rather some manner of duty-doing, some sort of aim, outside of themselves; these are the men of weight recognised and valued by their neighbours.

Redgauntlet,[1] as devoid as you please of amiable qualities, wins the reader's sympathy because he was

---

[1] *Redgauntlet,* Scott.

a man of will. He had the power to project himself beyond himself and shape his life upon a purpose. We may draw upon Scott without reserve for instances in this kind. The great novelist had a certain legal acumen which never failed him in his discrimination of character. As for his historical accuracy, mere errors of detail are, perhaps, fewer than we imagine; for the man who could deal with the case of 'Poor Peter Peebles'[1] knew well enough how to sift documentary evidence. I have already quoted two personages as figured by him, William de la Marek and Charles of Burgundy. Louis XI.[2] again, mean and unlovely soul that he was, was yet concerned, if meanly concerned, with matters outside of himself. What a fine study, again, we get of Will and Wilfulness in that crusaders' camp in *The Talisman*! Each of the princes present was engaged in the wilful pursuit of personal ends, each fighting for his own hand. And Saladin looked on, magnanimous of mind and generous of heart, because he was a man of will, urged towards ends which were more than himself. I can hardly conceive a better moral education than is to be had out of Scott and Shakespeare. I put Scott first as so much the more easy and obvious; but both recognise that the Will is the man. As for Shakespeare, the time will come when our universities will own a Shakespeare 'faculty,' not for philological study, but for what is beginning to be known as 'ethology,' the study of man on the lines of character.

**A Dividing Line.**—Both Shakespeare and Scott use, as it were, a dividing line, putting on the one side the wilful, wayward, the weak and the strong; and on the other, persons who will.

[1] *Redgauntlet*, Scott.          [2] *Quentin Durward*.

Faust, Lady Macbeth, King Lear, Edward Waverley, Charles II., King John, Marlborough, all sorts of unlikely persons, fall to the side of the line where Will is not in command. On the other side, also, unlikely people find themselves in company—Wolsey, Sir Thomas More, Laud, Mahomet, Henry V. of England, and Henry IV. Of France. The two Marys, of England and Scotland, fall to either side of the line.

To make even a suggestive list would be to range over all history and literature. Let me say again, however, that here is a line of study which should make our reading profitable, as making us intimate with persons, and the more able for life. The modern psychical novel is rarely of use 'for example of life and instruction in manners.' It is too apt to accept persons as inevitable, to evade the question of Will, and to occupy itself with a thousand little traits which its characters manifest *nolens volens*. The way of the modern novel is to catch its characters and put them to disport themselves in a glass bowl, as it were, under observation.

A man standing in the ranks cannot drill the company, and the restless forces of Mansoul can only be ordered by a Will, projected, so to speak, from the man, thrown to the front, aiming at something without; and, from this point of vantage, able to order the movements of Mansoul, and to keep its forces under command.

**'Will' may be a National Attribute.**—We are at this moment (1904) contemplating a magnificent object-lesson presented by a nation of extraordinary will-power; for this power may belong to nations as well as individuals. It would seem that every Japanese has an impersonal aim. There is that which he wills to serve with the whole force of his nature, and in comparison with which his tastes and inclinations, his desires and deserts, matter not at all. Who can doubt that he loses his life to save it, when, with purpose, method, forethought, every reasonable device, and with unlimited skill, the Japanese gives himself for his country?

Nor is this the first time in their history that the Japanese have given an example of will-power unparalleled in the annals of any country. Thirty years ago they worked out such a revolution as the history of the world cannot match. The people did not rise in arms and wrest power from their rulers; but the rulers, who kept the state and held the authority of feudal princes, perceived of themselves that the people had not room to grow under this feudal dominion, and they, of their own free will, retired from ruling and owning the land, from vast wealth and dignity, and became as citizens with the rest, served in the rank and file of the army, manned the constabulary force. These, too, lost their life, a princely life, to find it in the regeneration of their country.

The neighbouring empire, China, presents a curious spectacle of incoherence and futile endeavour. Yet China, too, has taste, literature, ingenuity, an art of its own, morals perhaps of a higher order than we Westerns suspect, the prestige of a long, long history; and, with all this, China is a petulant, wayward, unstable child among the nations. Why? We of the West are apt to say superior things about race and colour; but perhaps recent events have taught us better. Great things have come out of the East in the past, and may in the future.

The truth probably is that China and Japan rank themselves on the two sides of our imaginary line.

In the meantime, we Western nations have become enfeebled by a philosophy whose first principle is that we must never under any circumstances *lose our life*. The greatest happiness of the greatest number is our avowed general aim; comfort at all hazards is our individual desire; and 'Every man for himself,' is the secret, or open, rule of life followed by many of us.

But we need not be alarmed, and talk of deterioration and the like; nor need we compare ourselves unfavourably with any great nation. What is in fault is the teaching we have allowed and fostered, teaching which urges men along those lines of least resistance proper to their nature.

With an aim outside ourselves, we are as capable of great things as any nation of the past or present. If we are able for no more than little Skepsey's cuckoo cry, of his 'England,'[1] we shall be restored to the power of willing, which is only possible to us as we are moved from without ourselves. According as we will, we shall be able for effectual doing.

Our Lord's teaching appears to have been directed, in the first place, to awaken the Jews from the lethargy of national superstitions and personal aims; to give them the power of *willing* again; because it is only as a man *wills* that he is, in any full sense, a man. "What *wilt* thou that I should do unto thee?" "O Jerusalem Jerusalem! . . . how often would I have gathered thy children together, even as a hen gathereth her chickens under her wings, and ye *would* not!"

"If any man *willeth* to do His will, he shall know of the doctrine" (R.V.)

[1] *One of our Conquerors*, Meredith.

# CHAPTER III

## WILL NOT MORAL OR IMMORAL

**To 'Will' is not to 'be Good.'**—Perhaps what has already been said about Will may lend itself to the children's definition of 'being good,' and our imaginary dividing line may appear to have all the good people on the one side, and all the not good on the other. But the man of will may act from mixed motives, and employ mixed means. Louis XI., for example, in all he did, intended France; he was loyal to his own notion of his kingly office; but, because he was a mean man, he employed low means, and his immediate motives were low and poor. An anarchist, a rebel, may propose things outside of himself, and steadfastly will himself to their accomplishment. The means he uses are immoral and often criminal, but he is not the less a man of steadfast will. Nay, there are persons whose business in life it is to further a propaganda designed to do away with social restraints and moral convictions. They deliberately purpose harm to society; but they call it good; liberty to do as he chooses is, they say, the best that can befall a man; and this object they further with a certain degree of self-less zeal. It is the fact of an aim outside of themselves which wins followers for such men; the looker-on confuses force of will with virtue, and becomes an easy convert to any and every development of 'free-thought.'

It is therefore well we should know that, while the turbulent, headstrong person is not ruled by will at all,—but by impulse, the movement of his passions or desires,—yet it is possible to have a constant will with unworthy and even evil ends. More, it is even possible to have a steady will towards a good end, and to compass that end by unworthy means. Rebecca had no desire but that the will of God should be done; indeed, she set herself to bring it about; the younger, the chosen son, should certainly inherit the blessing as God had appointed; and she sets herself to scheme the accomplishment of that which she is assured is good. What a type she offers of every age, especially of our own!

The simple, rectified Will, what our Lord calls 'the single eye,' would appear to be the one thing needful for straight living and serviceableness.

**'Will' not the Same Thing as 'an Ideal.'**— Another thought that may occur is, that 'Will' is synonymous with an ideal: that the ideal, whether high or low, is the compelling power which shapes conduct. This is a comfortable doctrine, for most of us have an ideal hidden away somewhere, if it be only that of the 'good fellow' or the 'nice girl.' We see for ourselves the enormous force of *Bushido*, apparently the ideal of chivalry in Japan; but the ideal owes its force to the will-power which gives it effect. Everybody knows that the nursing of sentimental dream-ideals, however perfect they be, is a source of weakness. We know, too, that there are persons who make a cult of great ideals, who enjoy exquisite emotions in the midst of elegant surroundings as they contemplate and idealise the life of St Francis! Self-culture is accepted as the pursuit of an ideal; but when we realise that it is an ideal accomplished in self, and with no aim beyond self, we perceive that the gentle youth with the lily in his fingers and his head a little posed, is not a man of will, because the first condition of will, good or evil, is *an object outside of self.* Browning raises the curious question whether it is not better to will amiss and do it, than to persist in a steady course of desiring, thinking, feeling amiss, without strength of will for the act. Most of us who read *The Statue and the Bust* will agree with the poet that the fall which fails of accomplishment through lack of will is as bad as such fall accomplished. If it be not goodness, the will is *virtue,* in the etymological sense of that word; it is manliness.

Another thing to be observed is, that even the constant will may have its times of rise and fall; and we shall consider later one of the secrets of living—how to tide over the times of fall in will-power.

As has been said, a great secret of the art of living is to be able to pass the tempting by-paths and strike ahead. The traveller who knows this art escapes many torments; and this way of the will I shall invite the reader to consider later.

There are few subjects of thought more evasive than this of the will; but it is the duty of everyone to understand something of the behaviour of the will-o'-the-wisp who leads us. By degrees, we shall discover, that here is no *ignis fatuus,* but a power, working in co-ordination with the other powers of Mansoul, having its own functions and subject to its own laws.

Thus far we have seen, that, just as to reign is the distinctive quality of a king, so is to *will* the quality of a man. A king is not a king unless he reign; and a man is less than a man unless he *will*.

Further, we have seen that we have the choice of willing or not willing. It is even possible to go through life without an act of will. All that we do or think, in spite of ourselves, as it were, according to the impulses of our nature, is not willed. Will is neither virtuous nor vicious; but a constant will must have an object outside of self, whether good or bad. The will has, so to say, its times of high and low temperature; and the times of low temperature, of feeble will-power, are times of danger.

# CHAPTER IV

## THE WILL AND ITS PEERS

**The Will subject to Solicitations.**—It is rather easeful to think of Will standing before the forces of Mansoul, saying to this one, 'Go,' and to another, 'Come,' and to a third, 'Do this, and he doeth it.' The Will is subject to solicitations all round from 'the lust of the flesh, the lust of the eye, and the pride of life.' Every daemon of Mansoul tries, as we have seen,[1] to get the ear of the Prime Minister, and shows, with plausible reasoning, that he, alone and unaided, is able to satisfy all the wants of the State. From the mere greed of eating and drinking to ambition, that 'last infirmity of noble minds,' every single power of Mansoul will, if it be permitted, make for misrule. But, courage, my Lord Will! and the forces fall into place and obey the word of command.

We have already seen how the Reason firm, the enlightened Imagination, the ordered Affections, the instructed Conscience, are at hand with instant counsel towards every act of volition.

**Will does not Act alone.**—*It takes the whole man to will,* and a man wills wisely, justly, and

---

[1] *C.f.* Book I., 'Self-Knowledge,'

141

strongly in proportion as all his powers are in training and under instruction. It is well to know this, to be quite sure that we may not leave any part of ourselves ignorant or untrained, with the notion that what there is of us will act for the best.

Living means more than the happenings of one day after another. We must understand in order to will. "How is it that ye will not understand?" said our Lord to the Jews, who would only see that which was obvious, and would not reflect or try to interpret the signs of the times; and that is the way with most of us, we will not understand. We think that in youth there is no particular matter to exercise our Will about, but that we shall certainly will when we get older and go into the world. But the same thing repeats itself: great occasions do not come to us at any time of our lives; or, if they do, they come in the guise of little matters of every day. Let us be aware of this. The 'great' sphere for our Will is in ourselves. Our concern with life is to be fit, and according to our fitness come the occasions and the uses we shall be put to. To preserve Mansoul from waste, to keep every province in order—that, and not efforts in the outside world, is the business of Will.

# CHAPTER V

## THE FUNCTION OF WILL

THERE is, as we have seen, only one power in the Kingdom of Mansoul quite at its own disposal, a free agent, able to do what it likes, and that is *the Will*; and the one thing the Will has to do is to prefer. '*Choose* ye this day' is the command that comes to each of us in every affair and on every day of our lives; and the business of the Will is to choose.

**The Labour of Choice.**—We are usually ready enough to choose between things, though some of us shirk even that responsibility. We gaze upon two stuffs for gowns, and cannot choose between them. Indeed, the whole success of advertisements depends upon the fact that we wish someone, if it be only the salesman, to make up our mind for us. Some one has a rather clever story of a girl with two lovers, who was quite unable to decide between them, and one of the two made things easy by a pretended decease. The girl had no longer the labour of choice.

**We do as Others do.**—There are many people who minimise the labour of life by following the fashion in their clothes, rooms, reading, amusements, in the pictures they admire and in the friends they select.

We are all glad of a little of this kind of help, because it is well to do as others do in some of the small things of life; but fashion herself is a broken reed, and we must sometimes choose. The Joneses put off the labour of choice till the last minute. They inquired of their friends and consulted guide-books and weighed many considerations; but the more information they got, the more difficult was the choice of where to go for the summer holidays. So they went to the station, and trusted to the inspiration of the last minute; but, after all, Margate was a choice!

This inability to choose appears to be growing upon us as a nation, perhaps as a race; and the reason may be, that, though we are slow to elect for ourselves, we are zealous propagandists on behalf of others. We choose their furniture, their careers, their tastes, for other people, and push them zealously into that which we are assured is for their good. The gown may be becoming or the career may be suitable; but, in so far as we have chosen for another, we have done that other person an injury. We have taken away a chance from him or her of fulfilling the chief function of life, that of choosing.

We do a worse hurt to ourselves when we dress our persons in ready-made garments and our minds in ready-made opinions; because, in so far as we do so, we lose the chance of using our Will; we act as an automaton and not as a person; and no more fulfil our function than do the sham plants used in tawdry decorations. Every man and woman who does not live in the continual thoughtful exercise of a temperate will, is more or less of a lay figure, pulled by the strings of other people's opinions.

**Choice and Obedience.**—But you will say, 'What about obedience, then—to the home authorities first; after that, to the State, to the Church, and always to the law of God? If a person be truly a person only as he acts upon the choice of his own will, surely,' you say, 'obedience must destroy personality.' On the contrary, obedience is the exquisite test, the sustainer of personality; but it must be the obedience of choice. Because choice is laborious, the young child must be saved the labour, and trained in the obedience of habit; but every gallant boy and girl has learned to *choose* to obey father and mother, pastor and master, and all who are set in authority over them. Such obedience is the essence of chivalry, and chivalry is that temper of mind opposed to self-seeking; the chivalrous person is a person of constant Will; for, as we have seen, Will cannot be exercised steadily for ends of personal gain. But obedience must be given only because it is right.

Life, you will say, becomes too laborious if every choice matters, and is to be made at first hand. That reminds one of the fable of the pendulum that 'struck,' thus stopping the clock, because it counted how many ticks it must give in a day, in a year, in many years. The sum was overwhelming, and the pendulum stopped. The clock-face inquired into the matter, and the pendulum presented his big sum. 'Oblige me,' said the face, 'by ticking once.' He did so. Did that fatigue you?' 'Not in the least,' said the pendulum; 'but it is not of one tick but of millions of ticks that I complain.' 'But,' said the face, 'you are only required to give one tick at once, and there is always a second of time to tick in.' The Will is precisely in the case of the discontented pendulum.

No doubt there are many choices to make, but they come one by one, and there is always the time to choose.

**We choose between Ideas**.—It is well, however, to know what it is that we choose between. Things are only signs which represent ideas. Several times a day we shall find two ideas presented to our minds; and we must make our choice upon right and reasonable grounds. The things themselves which stand for the ideas may not seem to matter much; but the choice matters. Every such exercise makes personality the stronger; while it grows the weaker for every choice we shirk.

# CHAPTER VI

## THE SCOPE OF WILL

**Allowance does Duty for Choice.**—We have seen that the function of the Will is to choose, not between things, persons, and courses of action, but between the ideas which these represent. Every choice, of course, implies a rejection of one or many ideas opposed to the one we choose. If we keep the will in abeyance, things and affairs still present themselves, but we *allow* instead of choosing. We allow a suggestion from without, which runs with our nature, to decide for us. There would not seem to be much difference between the two courses; but most ruined lives and ruined families are the result of letting allowance do duty for will-choice.

It is not that a person need go through the labour of choice on all small occasions. A man goes to his tailor having made his choice; that is, he has long ago decided that the common sense and good taste of the class he belongs to are a sufficient guide in such matters. He remembers Lord Chesterfield's dictum; he will not be among the first to adopt a new fashion, nor among the last to follow an old one: therefore, his choice is limited enough, and his tailor sees to the rest. But, you will say, he has not chosen at all!

Yes, he has; he has chosen with modesty and good sense to follow the lead set by the common sense of his class.

A young man of more pretensions comes to his tailor and is shown the latest cut, a material that will be 'the thing' in a few months. He asks many questions, deliberates a good deal, or rather, invites his tailor to say, 'The very thing for *you*, sir! Lord Tom Foley ordered the very same thing last week.' That does it: the thing of a new cut or a striking pattern is sent home, and the young man considers that he has made his choice. Not at all: the tailor has played on his vanity, and his act, in ordering the garment, has been one of *allowance*, not of choice. He is but playing Malvolio after all! Another man visits his tailor, who takes his measure in more senses than one. This man is proud, not vain; he does not choose to set the fashion, but to be above it. 'I never wear' this, 'I prefer' the other, is the line he takes. The tradesman humours him, and the purchase, again, is not a matter of choice, but of *allowance*.

Or, again, there is the man whose conceit leads him to defy general usage and startle the world with checks and ties, feeling that he is a mighty independent fellow. He is merely obeying the good conceit he has formed of himself, and his daring ventures come of allowance and not of choice. We cannot follow the woman to her dressmaker's; the considerations are too complicated! But here, too, the decision arises either from *choice* made upon deliberate principles regulating taste and outlay, or upon *allowance*—the suggestion of a costume displayed in a shop window, or the insinuations of the tradeswoman as to what is worn and is becoming.

Once having arrived at principles of choice in such matters, the special occasions give very little trouble. A choice of will implies some previous action of judgment and conscience, some knowledge of the subject, and, generally, some exercise of taste and imagination. We do not choose a thing because we *will* to do so—that would be mere waywardness; but will acts upon information and reflection. The question of a lady's shopping is only a by-issue, but it is well worth considering; for, alas! the shopping scene at Madame Mantalini's is of too frequent occurrence, and is as damaging to the nerves and *morale* of the purchaser as to those of the weary shopwomen.

**Cheap 'Notions.'**—The dishonest fallacy, that it is our business to get the best that is to be had at the lowest price, is another cause of infinite waste of time, money, and nervous energy. The haunting of sales, the ransacking of shop after shop, the sending for patterns here, there, and everywhere, and various other immoralities, would be avoided if we began with the deliberate will-choice of a guiding principle; that, for example, we are not in search of the best and the cheapest, but, of what answers our purpose at the price we can afford to pay.

The mad hunt for the best, newest, most striking, and *cheapest*, is not confined to matters of dress and ornament, household use and decoration. We are apt to run after our opinions and ideas with the same restless uncertainty. Indeed, it is ideas we hunt all the time; even if we go to a sale with the dishonest and silly notion that we shall get such and such a thing—'a bargain,' that is, for less than its actual worth.

It is well to remember that in all our relations of life, our books and friends, our politics and our religion, the act of choice, the one possible act of the Will, has always to be performed between ideas. It is not that ideas stand for things; but things stand for ideas, and we have to ask ourselves what we really mean by allowing this and that, by choosing the one or the other. Are we going after the newest and cheapest things in morals and religion? are we picking up our notions from the penny press or from the chance talk of acquaintances? If we are, they are easily come by, but will prove in the end a dear bargain. We have expended the one thing that makes us of value, our personality, upon that which is worth nothing. For personality, the determination of the Will, is wasted,—not by use, but by disuse,—in proportion as it is not employed. We must bring wide reading, reflection, conscience, and judgment to bear upon our opinions, if it be only an opinion concerning a novel or a sermon—upon our principles, if they affect only the ordering of our day.

> "Who sweeps a room as for Thy law
> Makes that and the action fine,"

is a general principle; and no action is fine but as it reaches after a principle greater than itself. The ideas we admit become our opinions; the opinions upon which we take action become our principles; our principles and our opinions are ourselves, our character, the whole of us for which we are responsible.

One idea is free, one great will-choice is open to us all. We are inclined to wait upon circumstances and upon opportunities, but it is not necessary, nor, indeed, does it answer, for the person who waits for his opportunity is not ready for it when it comes. The great decision open to us all, the great will act of a life, is whether we shall make our particular Mansoul available for service by means of knowledge, love, and endeavour. Then, the opportunities that come are not our affair, any more than it is the affair of the soldier whether he has sentry duty or is called to the attack.

# CHAPTER VII

## SELF-CONTROL—SELF-RESTRAINT—SELF-COMMAND —SELF-DENIAL

**Moral Self-culture.**—The four types of behaviour now to be considered are not attractive. An instinct, perhaps a true instinct, repels us from all substantives compounded with 'self.' 'What's the good?' we say, when an ideal of self-culture is held up for our admiration, and the Will jibs. It is not to be moved to any constant action for self-centred ends. To be sure, as we have seen, a score of self-originated motives—self-esteem, self-respect, and the like—that come of vanity and pride move us to action, not against our will, but without our will. And the self-control and self-constraint to which we have been exhorted from infancy, and rightly so, even self-denial, may be practised and perfected, all for the sake of that dear Self which perceives that serenity is blessed, that self-approval is a happy state, that self-complacency is singularly agreeable to the one who has it; that, in fact, this sort of moral self-culture pays. Then, has not Self a right to be complacent on the score of such results; for, how they tend to the comfort of everyone else! How they make for peace and pleasantness!

**Self-Absorption.**—I am not sure. The moral self-culture which is practised for its own sake is apt to give a curious apartness to the self-cultured person. There is a loss of spontaneity, a suggestion of a 'higher plane,' which stops the flow of simple, natural sympathy, the only gift we have for one another. Any sort of absorption has this effect; no one expects much of a lover, or a poet, or of a student cramming for an examination; but the lover's case is, we know, only a phase, and so is the student's; and as for the poet, in so far as there is anything in him, he is working for the world. But nothing comes of self-absorption beyond that personal culture which is its aim. The rest of us are not very willing to be benefited by persons who are evidently on another plane: even Christ reached us where we are, for was He not in all points tempted like as we are?

I remember once meeting, amongst a large party, a lady who was rather a puzzle to me. She was striking-looking and very agreeable. She was a leader in whatever went on in the house—acting, reciting, games, talk—and excelled everyone else in whatever she did. She was very kind, too; wherever there was a little need or ailment, she was on the watch to give help. This lady was a puzzle to me, because, with so much that was charming, there was a certain aloofness about her that was repellent. I thought, perhaps she was a woman with a story; but, no, everybody knew all about her. At last her kind wish to help me disclosed the mystery. If I laid myself upon my bed in such and such a position, and said, 'I am very happy, there is nothing the matter with me,' etc., etc., for so long every day, the result would be perfect serenity of mind and health of body.

Then I saw what put this interesting woman out of touch with the people about her. She had a distinct personal cult, a cult of her own well-being, which, notwithstanding many kindnesses, proved like a wall topped with broken glass to the rest of us; we could not get at her, and though she practised every one of the behaviours at the head of this chapter, and more of the kind, I believe it was nothing to the rest of the party.

**A Better Way.**—Self-restraint, the ordering of our appetites; self-control, the keeping back the expression of our passions and emotions; self-command, which keeps our temper from running away with us; self-denial, which causes us to do without things that we want—all these may be excellent; but there is a better way.

When the Will aims at what is without self and more than self, the appetites are no longer ravenous, nor the emotions overpowering, nor the temper rebellious (except for a quick, impulsive instant, followed by regret and recovery). As for self-denial, it is impossible for love to go without what it wants, because it is not aware of personal wants. The mother who feeds her child with the last crust, covers it with her last rag, does not exercise self-denial, but love. Probably a great deal of harm to ourselves and others is done by what we call our self-denials. "I won't have you saving yer dirty sowl upon me," said an Irish woman to her district visitor; and it is just possible that she expressed a law of life,—that we are not allowed to be good to others, or even to be good in ourselves, just for the sake of being good. Love, and the service of love, are the only things that count.

Give the Will an object outside itself, and it will

leap to service, even to that most difficult of all service, the control of the forces of Mansoul. It is not by one grand *fiat*, but by many ordered efforts of Will, that we overcome those failures in self-restraint, self-control, self-denial, which are the misery of our lives, and which we know to be sin by the wretchedness they bring upon ourselves and others, and the separateness from others which they set up in our hearts. It is not self-ordering, but an object outside of ourselves, leading to self-forgetfulness and a certain valiant rising of the will, to which we must look for a cure for the maladies that vex us.

But, you will say, our Lord Himself has bidden us to deny ourselves. Yes, but He asks of us the self-denial of a disciple who follows his Master and denies himself in the sense that he has no self, for the love that constrains him.

# CHAPTER VIII

## THE EFFORT OF DECISION

**We shirk Decisions.**—I have attempted to show that the Will stirs at the touch of an uplifting thought. It may perhaps move in the train of vanity, greed, or the like; but, if it do so, it is a mere supernumerary; the forces of nature are strong enough to carry their ends without an effort of Will. They call, not for choice, but only for allowance. And, yet, there are many little wearing decisions to be made in the course of each day, to call upon the Will for which is like bringing a Nasmyth hammer to crack a nut. So we go on asking ourselves, 'What will Mrs Jones say?' 'Will Mrs Brown be there?' 'I wonder which side Holford will take?' and so on. We try to relieve ourselves of effort by imagining the decisions of our neighbours. This is a wearing process, because our neighbours are many and their decisions are various; and if we take any one man or woman for our guide, we are still thrown out, because circumstances are never the same for two persons. We are forced to act for ourselves, and so many minor considerations press upon us that, like the tired purchaser at the 'Stores,' we take, at last, the thing that is offered, for no better reason than that it is offered.

Indecision is perhaps a malady of the age, nor is it altogether a bad sign. It means a wider outlook on practices, opinions, creeds. Sir Roger de Coverley poses as our patron saint, invoked on all occasions: —there is so much to be said on both sides that we cannot make up our minds; and at last we make them up at a blind run, and find ourselves where we had never meant to be.

**'Toleration.'**—We admire this attitude of mind in ourselves, and call it *Toleration*, a sort of creed that may be summed up in this wise: 'There is so much of good in everything and everybody, and so much of bad in everything and everybody; and nothing, and nobody, is better than anything else, or anybody else; so where are you?' 'What's the good?' follows—of going to church, of troubling oneself to vote for this measure or that, this man or that, of troubling oneself about public questions, of offering truth to the ignorant "What is truth?" as jesting Pilate said, and as we, with a lift of the brows, repeat. 'Everybody's creed or opinion is no doubt the best for him, and why should we meddle? We have enough to do to look after ourselves!'

Even about that we need not take much trouble. Some of us have 'luck,' and some of us, 'Providence,' to make for us all the decisions that matter. This is the sort of unformed thought that goes on in the minds of many people to-day; and they wear themselves out with petty decisions and walk blindfold into great ones.

**'Providence' and Choice.**—But surely, you will say, Providence does fix the bounds of our habitation and guide us in our undertakings. This is no doubt a blessed and restful truth upon which every Christian soul reposes; but Providence does not save us from the effort of decision, for upon this effort depends the education of character; and 'our Father which art in Heaven' *brings up* His children. As the wise parent sees that his children are invigorated by proper exercise, so we may venture to think that Providence strengthens the children of men by giving to each opportunities for effort, chiefly, perhaps, for this effort of decision. For the will grows strong by its efforts, and the will is the man.

Ludwig Richter has a charming picture to illustrate 'Give us this day our daily bread.'[1] A mother is spoon-feeding two dear round babies seated before her with open mouths; behind, is a big brother with his slice of *schwarz brod*; a sower has gone forth to sow in a neighbouring field, and a bird follows in his wake for private ends. Here we have the story of providential dealings. The sower sows, the mother feeds, and God giveth the increase. But these do not wait; they work with open eyes and busy hands, and the good that comes to them comes on the lines of their own efforts.

**Opinions and Principles.**—But, though the labour of decision is part of that sweat of our brow by which we earn our bread of every sort; yet, if our decisions mean worry, fuss, anxiety, and fatigue,— whether it be about the buying of a yard of ribbon, or the furnishing of a house, or the choosing of a career,— we may be quite sure we have got off the right lines; that Will is in abeyance, and we are being torn in pieces by conflicting desires or affections.

The decisions of Will are always simple, because they have, for good or ill, an end in view outside of

[1] *Unser Vater,*

Self. As we have seen, no part of us works alone in a watertight compartment. Throughout our lives, Will has been busy, taking counsel with Imagination, Reason, Conscience, Affection; and forming, by degrees, those great decisions on conduct which we call *Principles*, or those upon matters of thought which we call *Opinions*. The opinions and principles are at hand for little and great occasions. Our business is to see that we are not distracted by manifold little movements of Self. Then our decisions are prompt and final; we are not fretted by wondering if we have made a mistake, or, if we should have done better by deciding otherwise.

We have done the best that is in us, with prayer if it be a matter of any uncertainty; and then we are sure that we have Providence with us, as the sower has, whether the immediate harvest be rich or poor. *We* gain, at any rate; there is more of us for the next time of action, and we go our way with added strength and serenity.

You will say this is no ready-made way to a quiet life. No; but in all labour there is profit, and without labour there is no profit, whether in things of the heart or of the hand.

# CHAPTER IX

## INTENTION-PURPOSE-RESOLUTION

**The History of a Resolution.**—A gentleman was walking on the shore of a southern watering-place with his invalid wife. His attention was attracted by a greater black-backed gull which had fallen dead on the sands; other sea things attracted him, and by and by a little promiscuous collection began to form itself. This swelled and swelled, and, as the collection grew, his knowledge of the objects increased. At last he had so many objects, and so well arranged, that the idea of forming a big county museum presented itself. He embraced the idea, and formed a steady purpose, and the difficulties in the way only strengthened his resolution to face all the labours of collection and classification.

Here we have a sketch of the mental processes which all persons who do things go through. First, something *strikes* them: the man on the shore would not have called the gull an idea; but that which struck him was an idea all the same, the idea of interest and admiration roused, perhaps, by the dainty beauty of the gull's plumage seen close.

Then followed that arrest of the mind upon the natural objects offered by the sea which led to the *intention* of getting more knowledge about them. The intention was probably a little vague and general, but strong enough to move him to action; he found the things and got the knowledge. Then the intention became definite. He had an end in view which he meant to carry through, a *purpose*; and then, in the face of difficulties, came the strong *resolution*.

**The Progress of an Idea.**—Another man, perhaps, read, in his boyhood, a history of Drake. He got out of his reading a certain sense of spaciousness, and of the chivalry that adventures all for love of queen and country. His hero is not always to be admired for his goodness, but his manly devotion to a cause takes hold of the neophyte. He has found it good to be at home in "the spacious days of great Elizabeth," and his reading takes that direction for many years. He knows the Elizabethan dramatists, statesmen, 'sea-dogs,' poets. His thoughts become coloured. There is a certain largeness in his opinions and in his conduct of life. He has an uplifting effect upon his neighbours. He helps them to see matters from other than the personal or parochial standpoint. He himself may have followed no more adventurous career than that of a doctor or a squire, but he brings the breeze of the uplands about him, and all his neighbours are the healthier. Of his sons, too, one is in the navy, one in India, and a third has settled in South Africa; all carrying with them the spacious thoughts, the impersonal aims, they got from their father. We seem to leave this man at the inception of what we may call the 'Elizabethan idea,' when he read his first story. The arrest of the mind and the intention came with the steady pursuit of Elizabethan literature. We cannot so well follow out the stages of purpose and resolution, but, no doubt, they were there, because the fruit of that first seed-thought perfected itself in his life, and it continued to bear in the lives of his sons.

Had the arresting idea come to him from the circumscribed, self-involved days of Queen Anne, he might have become a dilettante on the look-out for Chelsea teapots and Chippendale tables. He, too, would have an influence on his neighbours, for we cannot spare anything that has been; but his influence would make rather for the small graces than for the larger issues of life.

**Personal Influence must be Unconscious.—** This question of influence is, by the way, very interesting. The old painters pictured the saints with a nimbus, a glory, coming out of them. The saint with a nimbus suggests what seems to be a universal truth, that each of us moves, surrounded by an emanation from his own personality; and this emanation is the influence which affects everyone who comes near him. Generosity emanates, so to speak, from the generous person; from the mean person, meanness. Those who come in contact with the generous become generous themselves; with the mean, mean.

This sort of influence we cannot help using; it is unconscious, and belongs to our nature. We have no business with the influence that comes out of ourselves, and *have no right to try to influence other people*. We are, of course, called upon to give and receive reproof, counsel, instruction, as occasions arise; but these differ from what is known as 'influence,' in that they are above-board: the other person is aware of what is being done. Our business is to be good, and then our influence will take care of itself. What we must take heed of, however, is that we do not put ourselves in the way of the lowering influence of unworthy persons.

None of us can be proof against the influences that proceed from the persons he associates with. Wherefore, in books and men, let us look out for the best society, that which yields a bracing and wholesome influence. We all know the person for whose company we are the better, though the talk is only about fishing or embroidery. Probably no one is much the better for virtuous and pious conversation, what school-boys call 'pi-jaw'; but everyone is better for coming in contact with a sweet, wholesome, manly soul, whose nature is not only within him, but surrounds him, and is taken in as the air they breathe by all about him.

**Sources of Ideas.**—It is well to get the idea which leads to a resolution from such a source. It is possible that *this* idea may come as a seed-thought to some reader—may arrest his mind, form his intention, concentrate into purpose, strengthen into resolution—that, if he can do no more for the world, his shall, anyway, be a Mansoul from whom wholesome, and not unwholesome, influence will emanate. We may have other things to do; great philanthropic labours may come our way: indeed, all labours for the world are philanthropic if they are sincere; whether the writing of a book, the sitting on a parochial committee, the helping to make laws in the House of Commons. But no one need feel left out in the cold because his work seems to be for no greater a purpose than that of earning his living. That, too, is a great end, if he *wills* to do it with a single aim. He need not mourn that he has no influence; everyone has influence, not in the ratio of his opportunities, nor even of his exertions, but in that of his own personality. Mansoul is in truth a kingdom whose riches and opportunities are for whosoever *will*.

**Will, the Instrument by which we appropriate Ideas.**—But there are persons who never entertain the idea that presents itself, and who, therefore, form neither intention, purpose, nor resolution upon it— the persons who do not use their Will. And there are persons who deliberately will and choose to entertain harmful and injurious ideas; the thoughts of whose hearts are only evil continually, whose purposes, resolutions, are ever towards evil ends.

These several acts of the Will, intention, purpose, resolution, are not only possible to us, but are required of us. The Will is, in fact, the instrument by which we appropriate the good, uplifting thought that comes our way; and it is as we seize upon such thought with intention, act upon it with purpose, struggle, with resolution, against obstacles, that we attain to character and usefulness in the world.

# CHAPTER X

## A WAY OF THE WILL

**The Way of the Will a Slow Way.**—We have already seen something of the 'way of the Will.' We know that the Will acts upon ideas; that ideas are presented to the mind in many ways—by books, talk, spiritual influences; that, to let ourselves be moved by a mere suggestion is an act of allowance and not of will; that an act of will is not the act of a single power of Mansoul, but an impulse that gathers force from Reason, Conscience, Affection; that, having come to a head by degrees, its operations also are regular and successive, going through the stages of intention, purpose, resolution; and that, when we are called upon for acts of will about small matters, such as going here or there, buying this or that, we simply fall back upon the principles or the opinions which Will has slowly accumulated for our guidance.

We know that what we do or say matters less than what we will; for the Will is the man, and it is out of many acts of *willing* that our character, our personality, comes forth.

**The Will is Opposed.**—You will say, "This is all very well, and I should gladly choose to be among the men of good-will; but I know that sudden emergencies will overtake me, as they have always done before. Anger, greed, mean thoughts, the strong desire of favour here or friendship there, perplexity or fear, will come upon me with such force that I shall not be able to will or to do, but only to drift."

These sudden floods of the spirit—or the slow aggressions of outside influence—we are all sadly familiar with, and call them *temptations*; and we pray that we may not enter into temptation. But we forget that the mandate runs, '*Watch* and pray'; and, perhaps, three-fourths of the falls of good men and women arise from the fact that they do not know or consider at what postern they must keep watch. They strive against what they call their besetting sin, occupying their minds about that sin, in order that they may strive against it; and they so surely prepare themselves for a fall by this very preoccupation, that their story has passed into a proverb,'— Hell is paved with good intentions.'

**The Postern to be Guarded.**—The place to keep watch at, is, not the way of our particular sin, but that very narrow way, that little portal, where ideas present themselves for examination. Our falls are invariably due to the sudden presentation of ideas opposed to those which judgment and conscience, the porters at the gate, have already accepted.

These foreign ideas get in with a rush. We know how that just man, Othello, was instantly submerged by the idea of jealousy which Iago cunningly presented. We know of a thousand times in our own lives when some lawless idea has forced an entrance, secured Reason as its advocate, thrown a sop to

Conscience, and carried us headlong into some vain or violent course.

Seeing that neither Reason nor Conscience can be depended upon, once an idea has been admitted,—though they offer infallible tests at the gateway,—what we want to know is, how we are to treat insurgent ideas that press for an entrance. Fight them, say most Christian teachers; and the story of the mediaeval Church is a history of fights with thongs and lashes, hair shirts, fastings, and sore self-denials, shutting out all the sweetness of life. These terrific conflicts with evil, Martin Luther's inkpot, and the like, cannot, perhaps, be escaped when certain turbulent ideas have got in; but our Lord's merciful counsel of '*Watch* and pray' saves us. Given, the good Will, there is a means at hand, simple and unpromising against our giant, as was David's sling and stone, and just as effectual. In the spiritual as well as in the natural world, great means are always simple.

When the new idea presents itself in a newspaper article or in the talk of our friends—or rises suddenly in our own hearts—by a rapid act of the trained Reason and instructed Conscience, we examine the newcomer. We do this unconsciously; it has become the habit of the trained will (and the way to train the will is to exercise it) to submit the chance ideas that come our way to this manner of inspection before we appropriate them—let them in, that is, and make them our own.

Supposing they fail to satisfy the two janitors which coalesce to form our judgment, what then? Here comes in the beautiful simplicity with which the will works.

We do not struggle against, or argue down, or say bad things against the trespasser. By a conscious act of will, we simply and instantly think of something else—not something good and lofty, but something interesting, even something diverting;— what we shall do on our next holiday, a story we are reading, a friend we mean to see, even a fly walking across the ceiling, is enough to think about; because any other occupation of the mind keeps out the insidious idea we would repel, and it has no power over us until it has been *willingly* admitted.

Whenever life becomes so strenuous that we are off guard, then is our hour of danger. Ideas that make for vanity, petulance, or what not, assault us, and our safety lies in an ejaculation of prayer,—'O God, make speed to save us! O Lord, make haste to help us!' and then, quick as thought, we must turn our eyes away from the aggravating circumstance and think of something diverting or interesting: the weather, and the fitting garments for it, are always at hand!

We are all aware, more or less, that our moral Armageddon is to be fought against an army of insurgent ideas; but, perhaps, we are not all aware of the simple and effectual weapon put into our hands. Another thing that we are not all aware of is, that insurgent *intellectual* ideas have to be dealt with in precisely the same way as the moral insurgents within us. We are not free to think what we like, any more than to do what we like; indeed, the real act is the thought. Our opinions about God and man, Church and State, books and events, are as much the result of the operations of Will as are our moral judgments. They must be no more lightly entertained. Here is the need to watch and pray against the irresponsible flight of opinions for ever on the wing. Every such opinion must be examined at the postern, and, however attractive, if it fail to satisfy due tests, it must be pushed out of the way, diverted by some friendly and familiar thought waiting to occupy the mind. It is not that we must make up our minds beforehand to reject any class of intellectual ideas; but that it is our bounden duty to examine each as it presents itself, to submit it to the tests of Reason and Conscience; and, if it do not satisfy these, why—just to think of something else, really interesting and diverting!

An idea, once admitted, is our master and not our servant There are ideas, both evil and good, both moral and intellectual, which strike us, possess us, carry us away, absorb all our powers of body and mind, so that we may come to live, for better for worse, as the instrument of a single idea. How necessary, then, that we should keep watch at the door of ideas, and that we should become adept in the use of the simple means of repelling ideas we would not *willingly* entertain!

A careful study of the Gospels will show the vital importance of the ideas of the Intellect which we are apt to call merely a person's opinions—the opinions that 'every person has a right to form for himself.' Undoubtedly he has, both a right and a duty, but he should face his risks.

The Gospels are largely filled with the story of our Lord's controversies against fallacies,—that is, specious opinions proved by the Reason, and allowed to pass by the Conscience, because the Will permitted them unquestioned entrance. It is a perilous fact that Conscience and Reason themselves are at the mercy of an idea which they have not been summoned to examine *before* its admission.

# CHAPTER XI

## FREEWILL

**Summary of Points considered so far.**—We have seen that the ordering of Mansoul, the due co-ordination of all its powers, belongs to Will; that the Will is neither moral nor immoral; that the function of the Will is to choose; that the choice lies, not between things, circumstances, or persons, but between ideas; that an act of the Will evolves from long preparation, under the guidance of the Intelligence, the Affections, and the Conscience; that the operations of the Will are also of slow evolution, going through, at least, the stages of intention, purpose, resolution; that immediate acts of Will, which do not seem to go through any process of evolution, either in preparation or operation, are really only the application of principles and opinions that have passed through their due stages and issue in acts of judgment: it is these, and not the immediate decision, which are acts of Will.

We have seen, too, that many persons shirk the exercise of Will, the proper work of a man, and drift into allowance instead of choice, or into the wayward impulses proper to their nature. Intellectual opinions, as well as moral principles, belong, it appears, to the sphere of the Will. We perceive that the good Will, which humbly undertakes its functions in Mansoul, finds itself continually beset with hazards, impulses here, suggestions there; but that the field of action for the Will is narrower than it seems: Will must watch at the postern where ideas enter. This is the more necessary because Reason, a dependable guide as to ideas which the Will has not admitted, becomes a special pleader for an idea that has once crossed the rubicon—so much so, that there is no conceivable act of crime or folly that the reason of men has not justified to themselves by logical arguments, not to be refuted. Conscience, too, that other judge of our actions, is able to be convinced by Reason. Therefore, if Mansoul is to be saved from anarchy, the Will must keep incessant watch at the door of ideas. We have seen, too, that the obstructions to the rule of Will, arising from strong impulses and powerful suggestions, may be met in a simple way. The Will asserts itself, not by struggle and insistence, but by a diversion of thought, to be repeated as often as the impulse or suggestion recurs; and each recurrence is fainter than the last: whilst the Will employs the pause secured by such diversion to gather force.

So much we have been able to gather, more or less vaguely, about the functions and behaviour of the Will; and it behoves us to know all we can about this one practical faculty of man, because the task set to us is to work out our own salvation from base habits of body, loose habits of mind, inordinate affections, from debased and conventional moral judgments; and the Will is the single instrument by which we are able to work.

**Will and Conventionality.**—Our Will must
deliver us from the intellectual and moral fallacies
of which the air is full. It is by our Will that we
shall be saved from that commonplace respectability
which never errs, because every act conforms to the
standard of general custom; not by choice of will,
but in lazy imitation. This habit of life, though it
look like that of the man of good-will, is the despair
of all who care profoundly for their kind; because
the end of life—nay, life itself—is missed by all those
excellent citizens who live to save their lives; to do
well by themselves; to get on and prosper, that they
may have the more, whether of luxury, culture, or
pleasure. Life, circumscribed by self, its interests
and advantages, falls under the condemnation,—"He
that saveth his life shall lose it."

Therefore, Christ ate with publicans and sinners,
and pronounced woes against the respectable classes;
because the sinners might still have a Will which
might rise, however weakly, at the impact of a great
thought, at the call to a life outside of themselves.
The men at whom no one could point a finger were
tied and bound in self, and were incapable of the
great act of will implied in, "Choose ye this day
whom ye will serve."

There are but two services open to men—that which
has self as the end and centre, and that which has
God (and, by consequence, man) for its object.

It is possible, indeed, to choose the service of God
unconsciously, believing that we have only a passionate
desire to help men; but it is not any way possible to
drift into the service of God when our object is to do
well by ourselves: no, not even if that doing well
by ourselves reaches its ultimate aim—that of saving

our own souls. It has been well said that selfishness is none the better for being eternal selfishness.

If Christ were to walk amongst us to-day, perhaps He would cry in our streets, 'Woe to the land which upholds the standard of his own well-being as the aim of every man!' We cannot live higher than our aims. Will must have an object outside of itself, whether for good or ill; and, therefore, perhaps there is more hope for some sinners than for certain respectable persons.

We seem able to discern something of the function of the Will and something of its behaviour. If we would look closer and know what the Will is, if we would enclose it in a definition, it eludes us, as do all the great mysteries of life, death, and personality. This much we discern—that, in the man of good-will, the Will is absolutely free; that, in fact, there can be no will but a free will. Wherefore, the conventional person who makes no choice is without free-will, because he is without will. Will, freewill, must have an object outside of self; and the poet has said the last word, so far as we yet know:—

> "Our wills are ours, we know not how;
> Our wills are ours to make them Thine."
>
> TENNYSON.

# PART III

# THE SOUL

## CHAPTER I

### THE CAPACITIES OF THE SOUL

STEP by step, we have tried to gather together the little knowledge that is open to us about Body, Mind and Heart,[1] Will and Conscience. We have seen that no clear definition of either of these is possible, and that there is no rigid boundary-line between any two. The powers of Mansoul are many, but they are one; and, by careful scrutiny, we gather hints enough from the behaviour of each to help us in discerning those laws of our being whereby we must order ourselves.

We leave now the outer courts of Mind and Body, the holy places of the Affections and the Will, and enter that holy of holies where man performs his priestly functions; for every man is of necessity a priest, bound to officiate in his most holy place.

In every Mansoul, the 'Soul' is the temple dedicated to the service of the living God. How wonderful is the Soul of man! We commonly speak of ourselves as finite beings; but whoever has experienced the rush of the Soul upon a great thought will wonder

[1] See Book I., 'Self-Knowledge.'

whether we are indeed finite creatures, or whether it is not because we have touch with the infinite that we have capacity for God.

What is there that baffles the understanding of a man, or that is out of the range of his thoughts, the reach of his aspirations? He is, it is true, baffled on all hands by his ignorance, the illimitable ignorance of the wisest: but ignorance is not incapacity; and the wings of a man's Soul beat with impatience against the bars of this ignorance; he would out, out, into the universe of infinite thought and infinite possibilities. How is the Soul of a man to be satisfied? Crowned kings have thrown up dominion because they want that which is greater than kingdoms. Profound scholars fret under the limitations which keep them playing upon the margin of the unsounded ocean of knowledge. No great love can satisfy itself in loving. There is no satisfaction for the Soul of a man, save one, because the things about him are finite, measurable, incomplete; and his reach is beyond his grasp; he has an urgent, incessant, irrepressible need of the infinite.

Even we lesser people, who are not kings or poets or scholars, are eager and content enough in pursuit; but we know well that when we have attained, be it place or power, love or wealth, the old insatiable hunger will be upon us: we shall still want—we know not what!

St Augustine knew, when he said that the Soul of man was made for God, and could never be satisfied until it found Him. But our religious thought has become so poor and commonplace, so self-concerned, that we interpret this saying of the sainted man's to mean, we shall not be satisfied till we find all the good we include in the name, salvation. We belie and belittle ourselves by this thought: it is not anything for ourselves we want; and the sops that we throw to our souls, in the way of one success after another, fail to keep us quiet.

'I want, am made for, and must have a God.' We have within us an infinite capacity for love, loyalty, and service; but we are deterred, checked on every hand, by limitations in the objects of our love and service. It is only to our God that we can give the whole, and only from Him can we get the love we exact; a love which is like the air, an element to live in, out of which we gasp and perish. Where, but in our God, the Maker of heaven and earth, shall we find the key to all knowledge? Where, but in Him, whose is the power, the secret of dominion? And, our search and demand for goodness and beauty baffled here, disappointed there— it is only in our God we find the whole. The Soul is for God, and God is for the Soul, as light is for the eye, and the eye is for light. And, seeing that the Soul of the poorest and most ignorant has capacity for God, and can find no way of content without Him, is it wholly true to say that man is a finite being? But words are baffling; we cannot tell what we mean by finite and infinite.

We say there is no royal road to learning; but this highest attainment of man is for the simple and needy; it is reached by the road in which the wayfaring man, though a fool, shall not err. In this fact, also, we get a glimpse of the infinite for which we hunger. How strange it is to our finite notions that ALL should be offered to the grasp of the simplest and the least!

# CHAPTER II

## THE DISABILITIES OF THE SOUL

THE Soul, like the Mind and Heart, has its chronic disabilities, its deep-seated diseases. With an over-powering need of God, a great capacity to receive Him, common to all men, very few attain anything like a constant "fruition of Thy glorious Godhead." Many of us have fitful glimpses; and many, perhaps most of us, are 'unaware.' The causes of our deadness to things divine may be roughly classed under the three heads of inertia, preoccupation, and aversion.

**Inertia.**—We have seen how a certain lethargy of Mind withholds us from entering on the vast inheritance open to our intelligence. In like manner, the Soul is dead, and unaware of that hunger and thirst which God alone can satisfy. Conscience may be awake, may demand of us public worship, private prayers, the reading of good books; or, Conscience may be dulled, and we forgo these things; but, in either case, it is possible to have little or no apprehension of God—no wish, indeed, for such apprehension, for the lethargic Soul shrinks from that which must needs give it a great shaking out of its habits of ease. Such a Soul covets from other the praise that 'there is no harm in him'; from himself the praise that 'I do my duty' in all manner of proper observances.

The inner Soul is not dead; it could awake, if the Will of the man would respond to the approaches of the divine tenderness; but it is torpid—the cry, 'Awake! Awake!' does not penetrate the heavy ear.

The lethargic Soul is one with the wicked in this, that "God is not in all his thoughts." He is capable of living from hour to hour, nay, from day to day and from year to year, without that turning of the face of his soul towards God (as a flower to the sun) which is the sure indication of a living Soul. It is not that he never thinks upon God; perhaps there is not a man who never says in his need, 'God help me!' and perhaps not many who do not sometimes say, 'Thank God!' But this occasional and rare crying upon God is a widely different thing from having God in *all* his thoughts.

The hope for the inert Soul, whether he be a regular churchgoer or one of the 'careless ones,' is that some living idea of God may arrest his Mind and stir up his Will to desire, intend, resolve. This is what is called *conversion*, and is among the every-day dealings of the Almighty Father with His dull and callous children. We have all undergone such conversions, in a less degree, many times in our lives. And sometimes, to the generous heart or to the hardened sinner, a great conversion comes, which changes, from the moment, all the intents of his heart and the ways of his life.

**Preoccupation.**—As fatal as the lethargy of Soul which will not awake to the presence of God, is such preoccupation of Mind or Heart as leaves no room for the dominating and engrossing thought of God. "My duty towards God is to love Him with all my heart and all my mind," as well as "with all my soul and with all my strength." No power of Mansoul works alone in a compartment by itself, and Mind and Heart must unite in the worship of the Soul.

It is possible, and, alas! common enough, to be so preoccupied with one idea or with many that we are unaware of any need of God, practically unaware that *He is*. The preoccupation may be lawful enough in itself—praiseworthy ambition, family affection, or the passionate pursuit of knowledge; these are things for which we rightly give praise and honour; but any one of them may so absorb a man that he does not want God, that there is no room for God in all his thoughts, that the mere thought of God comes to be to him an encroachment upon thoughts he chooses to bestow elsewhere. He is not wicked, as men count wickedness, but he is living without God in the world. Though he does not know it, he is suffering a tremendous deprivation. He is crippled, mutilated in his best part, his highest function; and creeps through life like some poor wretch who spends his days and nights in a dark hole of a room, and never knows what it is to breathe in the open fields, under the broad sky. What joy for these, commonly generous, souls, to wake at last, here or hereafter, into the knowledge of God!

**Involuntary Aversion.**—But the Soul has another disability more puzzling and more astounding than either of those we have considered. There is in human nature an *aversion* to God. Whether it be,

according to the Article, that "original sin which is
the natural fault and corruption of the nature of
every man that naturally is engendered of the
offspring of Adam," or whether it is that jerk of
the shoulder from the hand of authority which belongs
to freewill, we need not stop to inquire. Anyway,
there is in human nature, as well as a deep-seated
craving for God, a natural and obstinate aversion
to Him.

The baby does not want to say his prayers, and the
ripe saint is aware of unwillingness, a turning away of
his thoughts and affections; and this, though all his
joy is in his God. This involuntary turning from
God is the cross and discipline of the Godward Soul.
But, from whatever cause it springs, it would seem to
be allowed in the nature of things; for, if our hearts
flew to God as inevitably as raindrops to the earth,
where would our election, our willing choice of God
before all things, come in? Where would be the
sense of victory in our allegiance?

**Voluntary Aversion.**—But there is a difference
between this natural, involuntary aversion, for which
we take shame; and the voluntary aversion, animosity,
malignity, towards God, set up by the rebellious and
sinful Soul; the Soul who, out of pride or open wickedness, cannot endure the thought of God, travesties
His Word, defies His Laws, abjures His Will, and
blasphemes His Name. When all this is done with
violence, we are shocked; but, when it is done with
an easy superiority and good-nature, and with power
of intellect, we are all, alas, too apt to swerve from
our allegiance, if it be only for an instant, and to
believe that the scoffer has more knowledge than we.
This is because there are in our own hearts the germs

of that aversion which he has nourished into a seed-bearing plant.

"Let him that standeth take heed lest he fall." Let us hold fast our loyalty, knowing that this, of making with our Will deliberate choice of God, is the only offering we can make Him; knowing, too, for our comfort, that involuntary aversion is not sin, and only gives us occasion for choice; but, when we *choose* to turn away, our sin does not put us without the limits of mercy, but it is immeasurably great.

# CHAPTER III

## THE KNOWLEDGE OF GOD

WHEN we realise how the Soul of man is disabled by inertia, by preoccupation, even by aversion, from apprehending God, we discern, at the same time, what is the great thing which the Will has to do; and it rises to a noble effort, to the uplift of a great thought. So long as we think that the things of God which we sum up under the name, religion, may be taken or left according as we have a mind; so long as we wait passively for sufficient persuasion, for a strong enough impulse, towards our chief duty, Will cannot sustain us. But once we realise that we have not only the world, the flesh, and the devil, but alien tempers in our own soul to combat; when we see that, in desiring God, we have set before us a great aim, requiring all our courage and constancy, then the Will rises, chooses, ranks itself steadfastly on the side of God; and, though there be many fallings away and repentings after this one great act of Will, yet, we may venture to hope, the Soul has chosen its side for good and all. The disorderly soldier is fined, imprisoned and worse—but he is not a rebel, and, when fighting comes, he does not desert.

We meet many people in the world whom we do

not know; some are too high for us and some too low, some too good and some not good enough; with some we feel we could have perfect sympathy, but they are too far off, we cannot get at them; while the meannesses and limitations of the persons about as make them unworthy, so we think, of the outpouring of our mind and heart.

But there is one great, perfect and satisfying Intimacy open to us all,—whether we are lonely because we feel 'superior,' or because we know ourselves to be 'poor things,' unworthy of much notice.

We are abashed when we think of the promotion open to every poor human soul. "This is eternal life," said our Lord, "to know Thee, the only true God, and Jesus Christ whom Thou hast sent"; and this knowledge, this exalted intimacy, is open to us all, on one condition only—*if we choose*. Feeling as we do that we ourselves are not good or clever enough for the friendship of some people, and are much too good and clever for that of some others, it is startling to know that this supreme friendship is to be had by each of us if he *will*, because every human soul has capacity for the knowledge of God; not for mathematics, perhaps, nor for science, nor for politics, but for that vast knowledge which floods the soul like a sea to swim in—the knowledge of God. The late Professor W. K. Clifford has told us of the agony with which, when he lost faith in God, he realised that "the great Companion was dead." The "great Companion" never dies. "He knoweth our downsitting and our uprising, and understandeth our thoughts long before," holds sweet counsel with us upon all we do and all we intend, cheers our dulness, rests our weariness, consoles our grief, gladdens our joy, chides, rebukes, chastises our sin, and gives us in ever-increasing measure that which all who have ever loved generously know to be the best and most perfect joy—the gradually disclosing vision of Himself. Like that blind man restored to sight, at first we see not at all; then we see men, as trees, walking; and then our eyes are fully opened to the vision of our God.

There are several ways by which the knowledge of God first comes to us; we may be struck by the words, acts, and looks of those who know—a very convincing lesson. A little plant of moss, the bareness of a tree in winter, may, as we have seen, awake us to the knowledge; or, dealings of strange intimacy with our own hearts, visitings of repentance and love, sweet answers to poor and selfish prayers, tokens of friendship that we can never tell, but most surely perceive, are all steps in this chief knowledge.

**The Bible teaches the Knowledge of God.**—But, as the friend listens to the voice, pores over the written word of his friend, so the lover of God searches the Bible for the fuller knowledge he craves. It matters very little to him that one manuscript should be superimposed upon another; that such and such passages should be ascribed to other authors than those whose name they bear; that not only the history, but the legends and myths, of the Jewish nation have found their way into the Book; that science disproves here, and history contradicts there: these things may be so, or may not be so. He is willing and thankful that science and scholarship should do their work, that the laws of textual criticism should be applied; at the same time, he sees a thousand reasons for caution and reserve in accepting

the latest dicta of the critics. He reads in his
newspaper how the King of Servia had twice to
remove the crown during his coronation because he
could not bear its weight, how the royal standard fell
during the progress to the cathedral, and how uneasy
these omens made the people; and he perceives that
the future historian of Servia, reading of these incidents, pronounces them legendary, according to all
the laws of criticism, and strikes them out of pages
which shall only contain history scientifically treated.

Little things like these give the Bible student
pause; he reveres truth and welcomes investigation,
but he also perceives that the latest critic is not
necessarily infallible. But all this is, for him, beside
the mark. If errors of statement, false ascriptions,
and the rest were found and proven beyond doubt
upon every page of his sacred books, yet he believes
that in these is to be found, and *nowhere but in these,*
a revealed knowledge of God.

Greece, Rome, India, Persia, China, unwittingly
affirm—alike through their poetry, history, and sacred
books—that men cannot by searching find out God.
A lovely gleam of the divine reaches one sage here,
another there; but each attempt to combine these
stray lineaments, and seize upon a complete idea
of the Godhead, has produced a pantheon here,
a monster there. And that, although the insight and
wisdom of the past have given us all the philosophy
of human life that we possess, every knowledge but
the knowledge of God.

In what are we better than those great nations of
antiquity who knew so much and did so much?
Only in this, that we inherit a possession vouchsafed
to the world by means of a nation whose spiritual

insight fitted them to receive it. We have a *revelation of God* which satisfies and directs every aspiration of the Soul of man.

Think even of the one amazing revelation,—that God is love:—

> "The very God! think, Abib: dost thou think?
> So, the All-Great, were the All-Loving too—
> So, through the thunder comes a human voice,
> Saying, 'O heart I made, a heart beats here!
> Face, my hands fashioned, see it in myself!
> Thou hast no power, nor mayst conceive of mine,
> But love I gave thee, with myself to love,
> And thou must love me who have died for thee.'"[1]

Here is a knowledge that men had never dared to dream, except as it is revealed in the Bible; and, yet, there are those who behave as one who found a huge nugget, and discarded it because the gold lay in a matrix of ore, and he would not take the pains to separate, and had no eye to distinguish, the precious metal. Such behaviour seems puerile in the eyes of the diligent miner. This is how the matter lies. The Soul is able to apprehend God; in that apprehension is life, liberty, fruition. Knowing God, the Soul lives in its proper element, full, free, and joyous as a bird of the air. Without that knowledge, "the heavy and the weary weight of all this unintelligible world" crushes out life.

But, fit and necessary as it is to us to know our God, it is by no means inevitable; indeed, as we have seen, the Soul in very wilfulness tries to evade the knowledge which is its health. We must begin with an act of steadfast will, a deliberate choice; and then, we must *labour* to get our best good, knowing that,

[1] Browning.

if we ask, we shall receive; if we seek, we shall find; if we knock, all shall be disclosed to us. But the seeking must be of single purpose; we must not be bent upon finding what we take for dross, whether in the Bible, in the ordering of the world, or in that of our own lives. Our search must be for the grains of gold, and, as we amass these, we shall live and walk in the continual intimacy of the divine Love, the constant worship of the divine Beauty, in the liberty of those whom the Truth makes free.

# CHAPTER IV

## PRAYER

**Unconsidered Prayer.**—It is hard to separate the functions of the Soul, because, indeed, all work together; but it is necessary to fulness of life that we should have continual speech with God, and also—though the soul is abashed before the greatness and sweetness of this hope—continual answering speech, These things are a necessity of that intimate union with our Father for which we are made. A hundred times a day our thoughts turn Godward in penitence, in desire, in fear, in aspiration, and—this is a truly delightful thought—in sympathy. Our hearts glow with delight at the blue of a gentian, the glory of a star, the grace of some goodness that we get news of: we lift up our hearts unto the Lord, though without a word; and the throb is one of sympathy, for we know that His delight, also, is in beauty and goodness.

**Response.**—These continual movements of the soul Godward hardly seem to us to be prayer, but they meet with response. We cry in fear, and hope is spoken to us; in penitence, and we breathe peace; in sympathy, and we expand in love. These are the answers of our 'Almighty Lover' to the dull, uncertain movements of our poor hearts. We all know how prayers for definite things have a thousand times brought answers which we have recognised; even the wilful prayer, which does not add, 'Thy will be done,' is not without its answer; the passionate heart is calmed; we learn to see God's way of looking at the matter, and are quiet.

Probably most persons who are seeking the knowledge of God would say, that, never once in the course of a long life has a prayer remained unanswered; but, that they have had in every case an answer which has reached their consciousness.

The walls of Jericho have fallen before them, the Jordan has been divided, their enemies have been smitten on the field of battle; and these things have come to pass in natural, unobvious ways, without any interference with what men call the laws of nature, but none the less supernatural, because they are over nature, above nature, ordered by Him who doth "refrain the spirit of princes," and "the hearts of kings are in whose rule and governance."

**Habitual Prayer.**—But, though there is this continual commerce between God and the Soul, the habit of prayer must be strengthened by set seasons, places, and purposes. We must give ourselves time to pray and times of prayer; rising early in the morning, we must seek our God and lay our day before Him, with its fears, hopes, and desires, in reverent attitude and with attentive mind. We must bring those who are dear to us for the blessing of our Father, and those in sorrow, need, sickness, or any other adversity, for His help. As the habit of prayer becomes confirmed, we shall be constrained to go abroad and help, while yet upon our knees.

Every record of war or famine, ignorance, crime,

distress, will quicken our prayers. As we pray, our love for all men will increase, and ways of help will offer. We shall remember our Lord's caution against using many words, for our God is in heaven and we upon earth; and, therefore, before we kneel to pray we shall meditate.

> "Ye are coming to a King;
> Large petitions with you bring";—

but they must be petitions thought out with purpose and winged with strong desire. Though—

> "Prayer is the breathing of a sigh,
> The falling of a tear,
> The upward glancing of an eye
> When none but God is near,"—

yet, we must not neglect the ordered and purposeful approaches to our God wherein the soul stretches her wings.

"Watch *and pray.*"

# CHAPTER V

## THANKSGIVING

**The Nine.**—"Whoso offereth Me thanks and praise, he honoureth Me," saith our God; and we are abashed when we realise that it rests with us to add honour to the Highest, and that we refrain our lips.

"Were there not ten cleansed, but where are the nine?" Alas, how often are we among the nine, the poor, pitiful souls who received everything and gave nothing, not even a word of thanks! It is worth noting that "the unthankful and the evil" go together in that list of lost souls which we find in the last book of the Bible. Even if we have our moments of thankfulness, when we cry,—

> "When all Thy mercies, O my God,
>     My rising soul surveys,
>   Transported with the view I'm lost,
>     In wonder, love and praise";—

our fault, and our very great misfortune, is, that we fail to take at regular intervals that survey of our life which must indeed cause us transports of gratitude. We fail to give thanks, partly because we are inert, partly because we are preoccupied with some fret or desire of the moment, and partly because of the petulant turning away of the shoulder from God which is our danger. But let us take time for the survey, if only on the Sundays, or, less frequently still, at the great seasons of the year.

'**My Rising Soul surveys.'**—How good is life, how joyous it is to go out of doors, even in the streets of a city! Surely a pleasant thing it is to see the sun! How good is health, even the small share of it allotted to the invalid! How good and congenial all the pleasant ways of home life, all family love and neighbourly kindness, and the love of friends! How good it is to belong to a great country and share in all her interests and concerns! How good to belong to the world of men, aware that whatever concerns men, concerns us! How good are books and pictures and music! How delightful is knowledge! How good is the food we eat! How pleasant are the clothes we wear! How sweet is sleep, and how joyful is awaking!

The Soul that surveys these and a thousand other good things of our common life is indeed a 'rising soul,' rising to the Father,—who knoweth that we have need of all these things,—with the gratitude and thanksgiving that are forced out of a heart overflowing with love. Even an occasional act of thanksgiving of this kind sweetens the rest of life for us; unconsidered thanks rise from us day by day and hour by hour. We say grace for a kind look, or a beautiful poem, or a delightful book, quite as truly as for a good dinner—more so, indeed; for it is true of us also that man doth not live by bread alone.

**We honour God by thanking Him.**—But we think so little of ourselves that it does not seem to us to matter much whether or no we thank God for all His surprising sweet benefits and mercies towards us.

Indeed, we should not have known that it does matter, if, with the condescending grace that few earthly parents show, He had not told us that He is *honoured* by our thanks! How impossible it seems that we should add anything to God, much less that we should add to His honour! Here is our great opportunity: let us give thanks.

Perhaps most of us fall on our knees and give thanks for special mercies that we have begged of our Father's providing care—the restored health of one beloved, the removal of some cause of anxiety, the opening up of some opportunity that we have longed for. For such graces as these we give ungrudging thanks, and we do well; but the continual habit of thanksgiving is more;—

> "Not thankful when it pleaseth me,
> As if Thy blessings had spare days,
> But such a heart whose pulse may be,
> Thy praise."

HERBERT.

# CHAPTER VI

## PRAISE

**Implies Discriminating Appreciation.**—If our dull souls are slow to thank, perhaps they are still slower to praise, because praise implies discriminating appreciation and reflection as well as thankfulness.

We know how the painter, the musician, writhe under the compliments of people who do not understand, while a word of discriminating praise sends them on their way rejoicing: they are honoured. This is the honour that the divine condescension seeks at our hands.

'We praise Thee, O God,' has ever been the voice of the Church. Prophets, confessors, the noble army of martyrs have, we know, praised God in their lives and by their deaths. To-day, there are those who devote themselves to lives of pain and peril for the honour of God and the service of men; and these too, we can understand, praise God. There are poets to whom it is given to utter some vital word, painters who present us with 'The Light of the World,' or, like the Russian painter, Kramskoi, with a vision of Christ seated in the wilderness. Such as these praise God, we know, but they are few and far between. So, too, do honest, simple souls who bear affliction willingly,

or who live their appointed lives with the sense that
they are appointed. All of these ways of giving
praise we recognise and bow before; but the duty
would seem to pass us by as incompetent persons.
We are not angels, we carry no harps.

But the duty of praise is not for occasional or rare
seasons; it waits at our doors every day. If we had
not been told otherwise, we should have thought it
presuming to believe that the great Artificer, like
every loving craftsman, delights in the recognition
by others of the beauty, perfection, and fitness of
the work He turns out. It is so good to know this
of our God; it draws Him near to us with the cords
of a man. The Psalmist knew that "the merciful
and gracious Lord hath so done His marvellous
works that they ought to be had in remembrance."
He was never weary of telling how, "the heavens
declare the glory of God, and the firmament showeth
His handiwork," how, "He feedeth the young ravens
when they call upon Him," how, "all the trees of
the wood do clap their hands." We all see these
things; but David not only saw them, but they gave
voice in his heart to a continual hymn of praise.
And he, who knew how to honour his God by giving
praise, was, we are told, the man after God's own
heart.

**Discoverers give us Themes for Praise.**—
Every age would seem to have its prophets, be they
painters, poets, or what else, whose function it is
to lead in the praises of the choir. To-day, perhaps,
scientific men are promoted to this high honour,
and what multitudes of praises do they disclose to
us! We call such men *discoverers*, and rightly so,
because the thing discovered is there, they in no

way produce it; but it is given to them to discover, to show to the rest of us. Every day there is still some new call upon us for wonder, admiration and praise, at the disclosure of some hitherto unknown and undiscovered great conception, mighty exhibition of the Power which every scientist to-day perceives to be behind all 'natural' operations.

Think of a ship in mid-Atlantic being able to communicate, without visible channel, with land a thousand miles away on either side; and that this possibility has been always hidden in the councils of the Almighty, and but now discovered to the man 'prepared'! What may there still be hidden in those councils, waiting till we are ready for disclosure? What amazing discoveries have been opened to us during the last few years! how the sense of the immanence of God presses upon us through all that which we call nature! "How excellent are Thy works, O Lord! in wisdom hast Thou made them all: the earth is full of Thy riches." "He that giveth thanks and praise, he honoureth Me." Let us not neglect to lift, day by day, our offering of praise to our God.

# CHAPTER VII

## FAITH IN GOD

**'Only Believe.'**—"My duty towards God is to believe in Him," my *first* duty, *the* duty of my life, without which other duties would not appear to count much.

'Only believe,' the writer was told as a girl, to her great anger and soreness of heart. If 'only fly' had been said, she could not have flown, but anyway she would have known what definite thing was expected of her; but 'only believe' carried no meaning. Of course she believed, as she believed that yesterday was Wednesday, the 5th of October, say; that there had been a Queen Elizabeth; that at least one Pharaoh had ruled in Egypt; these things, and thousands like them, she had never troubled herself to doubt, and believed as a matter of course; but—God?

Of course she believed in God in that way, but how could it matter? She was aware that such belief was no part of her life, and she knew of no other way of believing.

Some such perplexity, no doubt, tries many a soul to whom it is brought home as a duty that he must believe in God. *My* duty towards God, which I must fulfil for myself, which no one can do for me, and which others can give me little conscious help in fulfilling. No one can give me faith, but others can help me on the way to it; for, we are told, "faith cometh by hearing, and hearing, by the Word of God": that is, faith in God, just as faith in a friend, comes of knowledge. We trust our friend because we know him; because we know him, we believe in him. Faith, trust, confidence, belief—they are all one.

**Faith in Persons.**—To say that we believe in a person whom we hardly know even by hearsay—the Emperor of Korea, for example—would be to speak like a fool; but we do say we believe in this or that statesman, churchman, or what not Indeed, the whole government and finance of the world are carried on upon a vast system of credit, that is, mutual belief. We say, 'safe as the Bank of England'; but the Bank of England itself is conducted upon credit. We send members to Parliament to represent us because we believe in them. The members of a family believe in each other; and, should jealousy or mistrust arise between parents and children, husband and wife, it is an exception, a shameful exception to the general rule of confidence.

So, too, of dishonesty and venality in common trade and public trusts. Such things occur, but they are shameful exceptions; the general rule is that we live by faith in one another, and this common trust comes of common knowledge. Experience of the world and of life teaches us faith; and it is only the sour and ill-conditioned person who judges by the exception, and says with the Psalmist in his black hour, "All men are liars."

As there are two sorts of faith which we give to our fellows,—one, the general faith we give to men and institutions, which comes of general knowledge and experience; and the other, the intimate and particular faith we give to those whom we believe we know perfectly—the faith which is love: so there are two sorts of faith in God,—one, the general faith that all is ordered for the best, that God will provide, and that God will have mercy upon us.

If we wish to trace the work of this sort of faith, let us ask our hearts honestly if it means love. Does our soul spring at the thought of our God, crying, "I will arise and go to my Father," just as we have a heart-movement of springing and going at the thought of the person we love and believe in? If we do not love we do not believe, because faith does not come to us by accident, or even by nature. The faith we give to our friends is recognition of whatever nobleness and beauty of soul there is in them; and this is the manner of faith we owe to God, the recognition—born of knowledge—of Him who is Love and Light and Truth, Him to whom the heart cries, "Whom have I in heaven but Thee? And there is none upon earth that I desire in comparison of Thee."[1]

**Faith, an Act of Will.**—We have already considered how we may attain the knowledge of God, and faith is the act of Will by which we choose Him whom we have learned to know. Out of faith comes love, out of love comes service, and it is hardly possible to distinguish under different names the outgoings of the Christian heart in desire after God. "Like as the hart desireth the water brooks, so longeth my soul after Thee, O God":[1] there we have knowledge, faith, and love.

[1] Prayer Book version of the Psalms.

**Not Optional.**—The point I would urge is, that
this attitude of Soul is not optional; it is a debt we
owe, a duty required of us. To say that we do not
know that which has been revealed to us, to say that
we do not believe in a revelation the truth of which
bears the ultimate test, in that it discloses to us the God
whom our Souls demand, and in whom they find
perfect satisfaction, "whose ways are ways of pleasantness, and all whose paths are peace": to say this is to
commit an act of insubordination at the least, an act
of infidelity in the simple meaning of the word, worse
than infidelity to any human relationship, because our
God is more and nearer to us than any.

Men satisfy their Conscience that they have done
their whole duty when they do their duty towards
their neighbour; but what right have we to choose
a moiety of the law for our observance, the lesser
moiety, and leave the greater,—our duties of personal
knowledge, faith, love, and service towards our
God, which are to be fulfilled directly; and not
indirectly, through serving men. Both duties lie
upon each of us—*my* duty; and *my* duty towards
God is the first.

There is no space in a single short volume to
consider the articles of the Christian faith, even in
the concise form in which they are set forth in the
Apostles' Creed.

We say 'The Creed' glibly enough, and think we
understand it, until now one article and now another
is challenged by the sceptic; then, because we have
nothing to reply, we secretly give up one clause after
another, and think that we hold to the rest. It should
help us to know that not a single article of our Creed
appeals to our understanding. We know no more

about the Creation than we do about the Incarnation,
no more about the forgiveness of sins than about the
resurrection of the body. All is mystery, being what
the heart of man could not conceive of unless it had
been revealed.

"Great is the mystery of Godliness: God manifest
in the flesh, justified in the spirit, seen of angels,
preached unto the Gentiles, believed on in the world,
received up into glory." And what a barren and dry
land should we dwell in if our spirits were narrowed
to the limits of that which we can comprehend!
Where we err is in supposing that mystery is
confined to our religion, that everything else is
obvious and open to our understanding: whereas
the great things of life, birth, death, hope, love,
patriotism, why a leaf is green, and why a bird is
clothed in feathers—all such things as these are
mysteries; and it is only as we can receive that
which we cannot understand, and can discern the
truth of that which we cannot prove, and can
distinguish between a luminous mystery and a
bewildering superstition, that we are able to live
the full life for which we were made.

One thing we must hold fast—a clear conception
of what is meant by Christianity, It is not 'being
good' or serving our fellows: many who do not own
the sovereignty of Christ are better than we who do.
But the Christian is aware of Jesus as an ever-present
Saviour, at hand in all his dangers and necessities;
of Christ as the King whose he is and whom he
serves, who rules his destinies and apportions his
duties. It is a great thing to be owned, and Jesus
Christ owns us. He is our Chief, whom we delight
to honour and serve; and He is our Saviour, who

delivers us, our Friend who cherishes us, our King who blesses us with His dominion. Christianity would only appear to be possible when there is a full recognition of the divinity of Christ.

Let us cry with St Augustine:—

> "Take my heart! for I cannot give it Thee:
> Keep it! for I cannot keep it for Thee."

# Appendix

# BOOK II

## INTRODUCTORY

1. How is the body sustained, and how ruined?

2. With what powers fitted to deal with knowledge is the mind endowed?

3. What functions serve the same purpose for the mind as do the appetites for the body?

4. Name some of the virtues which belong to love, and some of those which belong to justice.

5. What virtues include the justice we owe to our own bodies?

6. Why are body, heart, and mind in need of government?

7. What are the governing powers?

# PART I

# CONSCIENCE

## *SECTION I.—CONSCIENCE IN THE HOUSE OF BODY*

## CHAPTER I

### THE COURT OF APPEAL

1. In what ways may conscience be figured by a judge in a court of law?

2. To what two or three facts does conscience continually bear witness?

3. Why is it possible for conscience to give wrong judgments?

4. What advocate is employed to tamper with conscience?

5. Why is it necessary that conscience should be instructed?

## CHAPTER II

### THE INSTRUCTION OF CONSCIENCE

1. Upon what teachers does conscience depend for instruction?

2. Account for the value of the teaching given by history and biography.

3. For the peculiar value of the Bible as our instructor in morals.

4. How does poetry teach us?

5. Why is the teaching of the older novelists and dramatists to be preferred?

# CHAPTER III

## THE RULINGS OF CONSCIENCE IN THE HOUSE OF BODY: TEMPERANCE

1. Give two or three examples from literature of intemperance in eating.

2. In drinking.

3. In taking our ease.

4. In day-dreaming.

5. What is Carlyle's counsel about work?

6. What principle underlies temperance?

7. Why may we not be solicitous about health?

8. Show that neglect, also, of the physical nature arises from intemperance.

9. Give a few rules for the ordering of our physical life.

10. Why is it necessary to have clear principles as to our duty in this matter?

# CHAPTER IV

## THE RULINGS OF CONSCIENCE IN THE HOUSE OF BODY: CHASTITY (*Part I.*)

1. How do over-fond friendships affect chastity of soul?

2. 'Yet how have I transgressed?' What lesson for our own lives does this question of the King (Edward II.) bring home?

3. Why are we not free to give ourselves without reserve?

# CHAPTER V

## THE RULINGS OF CONSCIENCE IN THE HOUSE OF BODY: CHASTITY (*Part II.*)

1. Cite some examples of sane and generous friendships.

2. What rules for self-government may we deduce in each case?

3. What two classes of friends claim our loyalty?

# CHAPTER VI

## THE RULINGS OF CONSCIENCE IN THE HOUSE OF BODY: THE FINAL UNCHASTITY

1. Show the effect of dalliance in devious ways.

2. What habit prepares the way?

3. With what monster of our nature must we dread to be at death-grapple?

4. Where does safety lie?

5. How may we keep 'a virgin heart in work and will'?

# CHAPTER VII

## THE RULINGS OF CONSCIENCE IN THE HOUSE OF BODY: FORTITUDE

1. Describe Botticelli's 'Fortitude.'

2. Name some points in which Isaiah sets forth an image of fortitude.

3. From two or three examples show that there is an element of tenderness in fortitude.

4. Show that Sir Kenneth in The Talisman offers an example of fortitude.

5. Give an example of fortitude under vexatious provocations.

6. Of cheerful, serviceable fortitude.

7. What of the 'black ribbon' when things go wrong?

8. Show that fortitude belongs to the body.

9. What is the apostolic injunction as to fortitude?

# CHAPTER VIII

## THE RULINGS OF CONSCIENCE IN THE HOUSE OF BODY: PRUDENCE

1. Illustrate the fact that 'imprudence is selfishness,'

2. Show that prudence is necessary in our affairs.

3. In the choice of our friends.

4. How does prudence act with regard to undue influence?

5. Show that prudence prefers simplicity to luxury.

6. That prudent citizens are the wealth of the state.

7. What does the simplicity of prudence allow us in our surroundings?

8. 'My servant shall deal prudently.' How was this fulfilled?

## SECTION II.—CONSCIENCE IN THE HOUSE OF MIND

## CHAPTER IX

### OPINIONS 'IN THE AIR'

1. What part of our living do we emancipate from the judgment of conscience?

2. Show the danger of casual opinions.

3. How does a fallacy work?

4. Give four rules that should help us in this matter of opinions.

## CHAPTER X

### THE UNINSTRUCTED CONSCIENCE

1. Show that, in everyone, conscience is persistent upon some points.

2. How do you account for moral instability, and by whom is it shown?

3. Show, by example, that a nation may be unstable.

4. Illustrate the danger of a besetting idea.

5. Indicate some of the perils of moral ignorance.

6. Show that undue scrupulosity is an outcome of ignorance.

7. What moral advantage, exactly, has the instructed over the uninstructed conscience?

# CHAPTER XI

## THE INSTRUCTED CONSCIENCE

1. Show, by some examples, that sound moral judgment is a valuable asset.

2. Distinguish between the power to form moral judgments and the power to live a virtuous life.

3. How are we to get the former power?

# CHAPTER XII

## SOME INSTRUCTORS OF CONSCIENCE: POETRY, NOVELS, ESSAYS

1. Show that the power of poetry to instruct conscience does not depend on its direct teaching.

2. Indicate the gradual way in which Shakespeare influences us.

3. To what purpose should we read novels, and what sort of novels should we read?

4. Why should essays be studied for instruction?

# CHAPTER XIII

## SOME INSTRUCTORS OF CONSCIENCE: HISTORY AND PHILOSOPHY

1. Why does history make great claims upon us at the present time?

2. Distinguish between the informed and the ignorant patriot.

3. Illustrate the need there is for some study of philosophy.

4. By what means should we reach our convictions?

5. Illustrate, by the behaviour of Columbus.

6. How may we distinguish a 'message' from a fanatical notion?

7. Give one secret of safety in matters of philosophy.

## CHAPTER XIV

### SOME INSTRUCTORS OF CONSCIENCE: THEOLOGY

1. Most people 'live a poor, maimed life.' Why?

2. Contrast our Lord's method of teaching with all usual methods.

3. Account for the fact that our Lord's sayings are 'hard' intellectually as well as morally.

4. They sit in darkness.' Who sit thus, and wherefore?

5. Where is the harm of occupying our minds about questions of criticism?

6. Have we any indications that we are declining from the knowledge of God?

7. What is the one vital question for us all?

8. When are the little religious books we use unwholesome?

9. What should we bear in mind regarding the authors of the Scriptures?

10. What may we look for in the lives of men as told in the Bible?

11. Show that the revelation contained in the Bible is unique.

12. What two laws would appear to regulate the revelations given to the world?

13. What reflections should safeguard us from the 'Lo, here!' of each new religion?

14. What is our hope of distinguishing between the merely human and the inspired elements in the Bible?

15. How may we discern the essential truth in Bible narratives?

16. Show that the disregard of life which shocks us in some of these is paralleled in our own day.

17. Is there any key to the mystery?

18. Why is it necessary to put away prejudices and misconceptions regarding the Bible?

19. What is the penalty of ignorance about God?

20. Show that the common notion of God as an 'indulgent' Parent is unfounded.

21. Why is every slight record of Christ in the Gospels momentous to us?

22. Name any arguments that present themselves to the mind of a Christian in answer to the statement that 'miracles do not happen.'

23. Show that the words of Christ are more amazing than the miracles of the Gospels.

24. Why may we not accept the modern tendency to reservation on the doctrine of the Resurrection and the Incarnation?

25. What is the peril concealed in trivial doubts?

26. What would you say of the temper which examines, and finally cherishes, every objection presented to the mind?

## CHAPTER XV

### SOME INSTRUCTORS OF CONSCIENCE: NATURE, SCIENCE, ART

1. Show that ignorance is a vice in regard to the things of nature.

2. In what two ways does nature approach us?

3. Show that nature is an instructor in our duty towards God.

4. That nature moves us to gratitude.

5. Show that preoccupation of mind has of late shut out this teaching from us.

6. What instruction has science for the conscience?

7. Distinguish between science and scientific information.

8. What duty is laid upon conscience with regard to science?

9. With regard to art?

10. In what spirit should we approach art?

## CHAPTER XVI

### SOME INSTRUCTORS OF CONSCIENCE: SOCIOLOGY

1. Why is it necessary to understand how other people live?

2. Why is casual help usually a hindrance?

3. What are the conditions of helpfulness?

4. In what sense is it wisdom to know ourselves?

5. What have you to say of the greatness of human nature?

## SECTION III.—THE FUNCTION OF CONSCIENCE

## CHAPTER XVII

### CONVICTION OF SIN

1. What is the office of conscience?

2. What convictions appear to be common to all men?

3. Show that religion is not a substitute for the instructed conscience.

4. Name three habits of mind, either of which may stultify conscience.

5. Show that the uneasiness of conscience testifies to sin.

6. How do our sins of omission affect us?

7. Show that the chiding of conscience is a thing to be thankful for.

# CHAPTER XVIII

## TEMPTATION

1. How does temptation come upon us?

2. Whence does temptation arise?

3. What is the secret of heroic lives?

4. How is a trusty spirit trained?

5. What is our part, that we may not enter into temptation?

6. Is it possible for penitence to become an error?

7. What is its due place?

8. What do you understand by, 'I believe in the forgiveness of sins?'

# CHAPTER XIX

## DUTY AND LAW

1. Why is it wrong to do 'wrong'?

2. What is 'wrong'?

3. In what various ways have people answered these questions?

4. May we excuse wrong-doing because it is 'human nature'?

5. Contrast the serenity of the enlightened Christian conscience with the uneasiness of superstition.

6. Why is it a delight to perceive and to fulfil the law?

# PART II

# THE WILL

## CHAPTER I

### THE WILL-LESS LIFE

1. Show that it is possible for conscience, love, intellect, reason, to behave whimsically and unworthily.

2. What power within us has the ordering of the rest?

3. Show that it is possible to live without the exercise of will.

## CHAPTER II

### WILL AND WILFULNESS

1. Show that wilful persons are of various dispositions.

2. What is the common characteristic of wilful persons? Give examples.

3. Contrast the behaviour of wilfulness and of will.

4. Give some examples of will-power and wilfulness from Scott.

5. Class a score or so of persons (in literature or history) on each side of a dividing line—on one side, the wilful; on the other, persons who *will*.

6. Instance nations that fall on either side of such a line. Why?

7. Describe the teaching which has weakened the will-power of Western nations.

8. What is our Lord's attitude in this matter?

## CHAPTER III

### WILL NOT MORAL OR IMMORAL

1. Show that *will* may act towards good or evil ends.

2. That a person of will may use bad means towards good ends.

3. Distinguish between 'will' and 'an ideal.'

4. What curious question on this subject does Browning raise?

5. What is the distinctive quality of a man?

6. 'Thus far we have seen'—what six points concerning the will?

# CHAPTER IV

## THE WILL AND ITS PEERS

1. Show that the will is subject to solicitations.

2. That the will does not act alone.

3. What is the business of will?

4. When exercised, and upon what?

# CHAPTER V

## THE FUNCTION OF WILL

1. What single power of man is a free agent?

2. What is the one act possible to the will?

3. Account for our increasing inability to choose.

4. Show the evil of ready-made garments and ready-made opinions.

5. Why may we choose for ourselves only, and not for others?

6. How would you reconcile the two duties of choice and obedience?

7. Distinguish between the obedience of habit and that of choice.

8. What is it that we are called upon to choose between?

# CHAPTER VI

## THE SCOPE OF WILL

1. Show how allowance may do duty for will-choice.

2. Contrast the behaviour of will and allowance at the tailor's, for example.

3. Is it necessary to make a choice of will, at first hand, on all small occasions?

4. How does the fallacy underlying the 'newest and cheapest' lead us astray?

5. What great will-choice is open to us all?

# CHAPTER VII

## SELF-CONTROL—SELF-RESTRAINT—SELF-COMMAND—SELF-DENIAL

1. What is to be said about moral self-culture for its own sake?

2. How does absorption of any kind affect others?

3. Show the difference between absorption as a phase, or for a purpose, and self-absorption.

4. Describe a better way than moral self-culture.

5. Show that what we call 'self-denial' is impossible to love.

6. In what sense does our Lord claim self-denial from us?

# CHAPTER VIII

## THE EFFORT OF DECISION

1. How do we try to escape the effort of decision?

2. Sum up the sort of creed held in the name of 'Toleration.'

3. Describe a picture of Ludwig Richter's showing how 'Providence' and 'freewill' co-operate.

4. How may we distinguish a decision of will from one of 'allowance'?

5. What two assets does the person who uses his will gather through his life?

6. Show how these serve him on small and great occasions.

# CHAPTER IX

## INTENTION—PURPOSE—RESOLUTION

1. Give two or three examples of the history of resolution.

2. What truth is figured by the nimbus of the pictured saint?

3. When does 'influence' become injurious?

4. From what sort of influence must we safeguard ourselves?

5. The influence of a person is in the ratio of—?

6. What several acts of the will are required of us?

# CHAPTER X

## A WAY OF THE WILL

1. Sum up the conclusions arrived at so far with regard to the will.

2. What is to be said to persons of good-will who dread temptation?

3. Particularise the postern to be guarded.

4. The porters on guard.

5. Shall we fight or run away?

6. In what 'way of the will' does our safety lie?

7. Show that the same rule (what rule?) applies to intellectual and moral insurgent ideas.

8. Show how our Lord's condemnation of fallacies proves that opinions are judged upon moral grounds.

# CHAPTER XI

## FREEWILL

1. Why is it important to know all we can about the behaviour of the will?

2. Sum up (again) the sixteen, or so, points we have endeavoured to make, so far.

3. Distinguish between the man of good-will and the conventional person.

4. What two services are open to men?

5. What is the distinguishing mark of freewill?

6. 'The poet has said the last word'; what is it?

# PART III

# THE SOUL

## CHAPTER I

### THE CAPACITIES OF THE SOUL

1. 'We wonder whether we are indeed finite creatures'; give four or five grounds for such wonder.

2. Show the limiting and deceptive nature of our ordinary religious thoughts.

3. Show in what respect the needs of the soul are satisfied by God alone.

## CHAPTER II

### THE DISABILITIES OF THE SOUL

1. Name some of the chronic disabilities of the soul.

2. How may we discern in ourselves 'the inert soul'?

3. What is the cure of this soul-ailment?

4. How does preoccupation affect our relations with God?

5. Show how our 'involuntary aversion' to God may really be of service.

6. Distinguish between voluntary and involuntary aversion.

7. Show the supreme importance of will-choice.

# CHAPTER III

## THE KNOWLEDGE OF GOD

1. What is the condition on which we may have the one satisfying intimacy?

2. What persons have capacity for this intimacy?

3. What tokens of the divine friendship may we look for?

4. Name some of the ways by which the knowledge of God may first come to us.

5. Show that the Bible is the immediate source of such knowledge.

6. In what respect does the Bible stand alone among the great writings of the past?

7. Show how fit and necessary the knowledge of God is to the soul of man.

8. Is this knowledge inevitable?

# CHAPTER IV

## PRAYER

1. Describe some of the movements of unconsidered prayer.

2. Some of the responses to these.

3. What two requirements of the soul are thus met?

4. What are some of the uses and occasions of habitual prayer?

5. How may we serve the world in our habitual prayers?

# CHAPTER V

## THANKSGIVING

1. What causes restrain us from the gratitude we owe?

2. 'My rising soul surveys'—what occasions for being thankful?

3. For what, besides our 'meat,' may we well 'say grace'?

4. Why does it matter that we should thank God?

# CHAPTER VI

## PRAISE

1. Show that 'praise' implies more than thanksgiving.

2. Whom do we think of as being endowed with the right to praise God?

3. Show that 'praise' is our duty also.

4. Name some occasions of praise discovered by the Psalmist.

5. What persons, to-day, especially afford us themes for praise?

# CHAPTER VII

## FAITH IN GOD

1. Why do we find it perplexing to be told we must 'believe in God'?

2. How does faith come?

3. Show that we have faith in each other.

4. That there are two sorts of faith in persons.

5. Show that faith of both sorts is due to God.

6. How shall we know if we have the faith of recognition?

7. Show that faith is an act of will.

8. Show that to believe in God is a duty required of us.

9. Is this duty fulfilled in the service of men?

10. Show that no article of the Christian (or of the Apostles') Creed appeals to our understanding.

11. That all the great things of life also are mysteries.

12. Show that Christianity means the recognition of Christ.

# Index

## BOOK II.

As frequent mention has been made of the *Parents' National Educational Union* and its various agencies, it may be well to add that information about these may be had from the Secretary. The "*Questions for the Use of Readers*" are inserted with a view to the P.N.E.U. READING COURSE. Persons who wish to become "Qualified Members" of the Union by undertaking this course should communicate with the Secretary, 26 Victoria. Street, London, S.W.